This book belongs to

Marion Houghton
114 Prospect St
South Orange, NJ 07079

CRACKING UP

Christopher Bollas

CRACKING UP

The Work

of Unconscious

Experience

HILL AND WANG

A division of Farrar, Straus and Giroux

New York

From Buried Secrets by Edward Humes. Copyright © 1991 by
Edward Humes. Used by permission of Dutton Signet, a division of
Penguin Books USA Inc.
Excerpt from "East Coker" in Four Quartets, copyright 1943 by
T. S. Eliot and renewed 1971 by Esme Valerie Eliot, reprinted by
permission of Harcourt Brace & Company and Faber and Faber.
Thirteen lines from "A Primitive Like an Orb" and three lines from
"The Snow Man" from Collected Poems by Wallace Stevens.
Copyright 1948 by Wallace Stevens. Reprinted by permission of
Alfred A. Knopf, Inc.

ACKNOWLEDGMENTS

I want to thank Adam Phillips, Nina Farhi, Victoria Hamilton,
Ed Corrigan, Pearl-Ellen Gordon, and Arne Jemstedt for their
critical comments; Alison Wertheimer and Sally Singer for
valued editorial help; and Linda Mason for her assistance in
preparing the manuscript.
I am especially grateful to my editor at Hill and Wang,
Elisabeth Sifton, for her critical common sense, editorial skill,
and gracious support.

Contents

CRACKING UP

Introduction

This book examines the place of unconscious work in the psychic context of self experience, a venture I began in *Being a Character*, where I argued that Freud's vision of the total dream process is a model of all unconscious experiencing. That process, which starts with a sequence of psychically intense experiences during the day, continues with the dream "event," followed by cracking up the dream contents through free association.

To dream is to be dreamed is to be part of a dreaming, which carries on endlessly in a pairing of two quite different mental processes: bringing unconscious ideas together into a dream event and breaking them up through free association. Together they reveal to a psychoanalyst certain latent unconscious themes. But, equally important, they provide evidence of the freely moving work of the unconscious, which I term "unconscious freedom." This freedom is found in the necessary opposition between the part of us that finds truth by uniting disparate ideas (i.e., "condensation") and the part of us that finds the truth by breaking up those unities.

Freud stressed how free association reveals patterns that, he believed, derived from latent ideas not presented in the manifest content of a dream. But a dream will be weighty with hundreds of ideas, and fragmenting its unity through free association will not only show the hidden unconscious truths (some of which may be revealed by conscious inquiry) but raise potentially endless questions about diverse and disparate issues.

Through the method of psychoanalysis, Freud gave the analysand a place to present his dream in the presence of another person and a formal method of dissemination. Whatever important truths were found in a psychoanalysis that would facilitate a cure of symptoms and pathological structures, exercising this unconscious freedom in the presence of the other was deeply curative in its own right.

Though the total dream process is perhaps the clearest way of examining the nature of unconscious freedom as I have defined it, the same process can occur all the time, albeit on a much smaller scale. During the day, we have hundreds of psychically intense experiences when we conjure ideas from an inner medley of body experience, unconscious memories, and instinctual response. Each experience is fragmented by the associations it conjures up: we bring together many factors only to find that whatever lucid ideas we have are broken up in the process. Psychic life during an ordinary day, then, is an endless sequence of psychic intensities and their subsequent fragmentations.

This procedure is the rhythm of unconscious mental activity, and it constitutes the creative workings of the self. I use the term "creative" in a morally neutral and strictly psychological sense, for such freedom of inner movement may as easily be devoted to the workings of a fascist mentality as it could be to the development of a novel, the writing of a symphony, or the construction of an idea in ordinary conversation.

This process—of collecting condensations which in turn serve as the material of disseminative scattering—is vital to individual unconscious creativity in living. If a person has been fortunate enough to develop this capability, then he will develop in turn a "separate sense," which evolves from a certain kind of unconscious development and is part of the function of unconscious intuition. However, this kind of inner experiencing may be impossible for an individual whose life is dominated by a trauma, whatever its source. An obsessive-compulsive patient who upon entering a supermarket is not only prey to inner commands that he remove, let us say, all the tins of asparagus from the shelf but also victim of the demand that in fact he do so, is clearly caught up in an unconscious formation that may very well derive from both his instinctual history and his early traumatic experiences. Either way, he is not free to exercise an unconscious freedom; indeed, he may fear the part of his mind that operates outside his will, as it seems all too easy for it to get him in serious trouble. Thus, people who live inside the structure of a pathology rather than as comparatively free spirits will have altogether different "separate senses." Their intuitions will arise out of defective knowledge of the terms of their own fate, and although they may become exquisitely sensitive to certain structures in life, their intuition will express and often echo the traumas imposed upon them.

Unconscious freedom, as opposed to unconscious imprisonment, raises important issues about the nature and therapeutic effect of unconscious communication.

Freud's views on the nature of unconscious communication are both puzzling and provocative. My first chapter takes Freud's challenge seriously, asking how we can understand unconscious communication in terms of a theory of the unconscious which *theoretically* makes such communication an impossibility. If the work of the unconscious distorts the representations of unconscious mental content, and fools consciousness, then why and how does it convey these unconscious contents to another person?

Chapter 2 explores the psychology of the uncanny, and examines how people in intimate relations (including psychoanalysis) educate one another in the precise idioms of their unconscious lives—an instruction that develops a separate sense and enhances empathy, intuition, and unconscious communication.

Chapter 3 discusses the ordinary flow of unconsciousness in everyday life, especially that of what we call dissemination, when we creatively fragment along the lines of thought inspired by an intense experience, and Chapter 4 considers the person who refuses this rhythm of unconscious life and forecloses it through self-absorbing obsessions, preoccupations, and passions.

In Chapter 5, on the functions of history, I examine why the notion we each have of the "past" is ironic: rather than signifying something meaningful, it represents the death of our lived experiences, and our nostalgia for the past is a form of grief that is built into the structure of our concept of the past. Yet history can be understood as a creative transformation of the past, and, I argue, this changes the fundamentally traumatic effect of the loss of lived experience into meaning.

Chapter 6 asks: What is the self? Why do we use this term, especially as it seems to defy anything like a coherent meaning? Nonetheless, I explore what I think it signifies, arguing that the sense of self develops over time and develops its own capability—just as learning to write music eventually makes it possible to compose symphonies—and this can teach us a great deal about the separate sense that is the unconscious.

Chapter 7 examines a very precise unconscious structure that has always been linked to evil but has, curiously enough, been obscured by the evocative power of the very word "evil." I explore the work of trauma and the development of a malignant separate sense, one that registers the shadow of the object that has crushed the self, giving an acute understanding not only of the form of the other but of the manner in which fate intervenes to devastating effect. Identification of the structure of evil and of the person who identifies with it may contribute to our study of serial killers and others who seek victims.

The final chapter examines a sense of humor, which, it is argued, derives from the mother's ability to transform the infant's ordinary misery into amusement. Mothers "crack up" their babies, thus establishing a precedent for other types of cracking up, such as the one that occurs when the self breaks down in a dream or the deconstruction of speech in the process of free association.

1

Communications of the Unconscious

In 1914, a seventeen-year-old boy was referred to Sándor Ferenczi because he "had an insufferable voice" which doctors treating him had attributed to nervousness. Ferenczi found that the young man spoke in what was obviously a rather irritating "hoarse falsetto," and having asked if the boy could speak in another voice, was startled to discover that he then talked in "so deep a bass" that his voice "rang full and sonorous." When Ferenczi conferred with the mother, she indicated that she could not stand his bass sound, and would promptly intervene by saying, "I cannot endure that voice; you must learn to drop it" (108). The child obliged, thus also dropping his masculine identification, unconsciously obeying his mother's prohibition against what she unconsciously perceived as his incestuous strivings. "In my opinion," Ferenczi wrote, "we have to do here with one of those numerous cases that I am in the habit of calling Dialogues of the Unconscious, in which the unconscious of two people completely understand themselves and each other, without the remotest conception of this on the part of the consciousness of either" (109).

In a startling and far-reaching metaphor, Freud likened the analyst's reception of the patient's unconscious to a radio set receiving a transmission. "He must turn his own unconscious like a receptive organ toward the transmitting unconscious of the patient. He must adjust himself to the patient as a telephone receiver is adjusted to the transmitting microphone. Just as the receiver converts back into sound waves the electric oscillations in the telephone line which were set up by sound waves, so the doctor's unconscious is able, from the derivatives of the unconscious which are communicated to him, to reconstruct that unconscious, which has determined the patient's free associations" (1912, 115–16).

Freud's statement is clear, but puzzling. What particular part of the analyst's—and presumably anyone's—unconscious can function as a receiver-translator? How does this work?

He provides certain clues in his seminal paper "The Unconscious," where he writes: "It is a very remarkable thing that the *Ucs.* of one human being can react upon that of another, without passing through the *Cs.* This deserves closer investigation, especially with a view to finding out whether preconscious activity can be excluded as playing a part in it; but descriptively speaking, the fact is incontestable." This comment follows immediately after—i.e., in free narrative association to—his statement that the unconscious *is directly affected* by external experiences rather than mediated through the preconscious. "The *Ucs.* is also affected by experiences originating from external perception. Normally all the paths from perception to the *Ucs.* remain open, and only those leading from the *Ucs.* are subject to blocking by repression" (1915, 194). In other words the unconscious can receive experiences from external reality, and presumably—given his free association—it can also receive the other's unconscious without preconscious intermediation.

The classical psychoanalyst regards his patient's associations as a chain of ideas that eventually reveals moving trains of thought traveling in a sequential logic of association; when he discovers an unconscious idea buried in the chain he may render it conscious through interpretation, but since he believes the patient's free associations to be a moving manifest text, can he claim consistently to decipher the latent ideas that drive the signifiers *in situ*? Would this not amount to a deconstructive capacity which "knows" how to work the sender's message by following its displacements, condensations, and substitutions? Could one person unconsciously track another like this? Such a vigilant effort of deconstructive connectedness hardly seems a property of the Freudian unconscious except as a rationalizing device to create a pseudo-meaning for the dream experience, in order to keep the dreamer asleep.

In fact, the analyst makes no such claim, being content to pursue only those latent ideas he perceives over time; indeed, experienced analysts of the same school of thought listening to the same chain of ideas would disagree over its latent meaning, and the same clinician may hear things differently according to his changing frames of mind. The analyst's conscious grasp of the patient's latent ideas is often as unconsciously determined as the patient's own associations. Unconscious communication always takes place between two minds that process one another according to the dream work. So the movement which constitutes the specific *workings* of the unconscious will not be available to consciousness, although specific mental contents may be.

The analyst listening to the patient's chain of ideas in that special frame of mind that is characterized by evenly hovering attentiveness is not engaged in a form of deconstructive vigilance: as Freud implies, the analyst free-associates to his patient, drifting *away* through associative pathways of his own, riding the patient's narrative, sometimes like a child following a storytelling parent, or a scientist stopping to ponder a thing or two before catching up again. An idea, an image, a word falls out of the blue —what Freud termed *Einfall* (a mental content that simply drops in uninvited by consciousness)—and often these are riotously anticontextual. This complex psychic movement—a kind of *countertransference dreaming*—reflects the analyst's consistent topographical response as he transforms the patient's material according to the laws of the dream work: displacing the patient's narrative into a counternarrative, condensing the patient's descriptions with this patient's other accounts, incorporating the analysand's mood into his own emotional constellation, altering an image or changing a word, bearing the analysand's psychic state within his own body, thus creating his own somatic double to the patient.

Freud's unconscious receiver, the dream set of countertransference, processes the patient's unconscious communications on its own terms: one dreamer to another. Dreaming the analysand during the hour, bringing the patient to another place, transformed into other persons, events, and places, the analyst *unconsciously* deconstructs —displaces, condenses, substitutes the patient.

As unconscious thinking knows no contradictions and opposing ideas easily coexist, and as the unconscious ignores time, with moments in early childhood represented alongside contemporary events, internal social possibilities are radicalized in a dream: people whom the dreamer knew but who never met one another can be companions in the dream. Listening to the material as an unconscious attendant, the analyst entertains many contradictory ideas about a patient. This is, of course, inevitable given the length, complexity, and intimacy of the relationship. Thinking of something the patient said the previous week, recalling an image reported months before, struck by an interpretation delivered sometime in the early years of the analysis, an analyst is time-warped, too, his conscious thought processes dispersed by unconscious thinking. As he carries evolving contradictions and condenses events from differing periods of the analysis, he is *recurrently confused*, wandering in the strange country of even suspension.

Recounting a trip to the south of Italy to visit his sister, a patient describes to me the small town she lives in. He muses on his nephew, who is six. He ponders his sister's unhappy marriage, punctuating his story with many asides as he recalls various things she did, such as cooking pasta with tomatoes from her garden. The description of the meal reminds me of a dream he once had about collecting tomatoes on a city street, which in turn evokes within me a brief condensed image of an orange grove in southern California and a house where a beautiful girl lived, and I am suddenly aware of romantic feelings toward my patient's sister, which I know must represent my feelings for him. Didn't he tell me that his nephew was named after their father? Isn't this the boy who was in hospital some six weeks ago? I think so; but there is no report of that in this account, although it is on my mind. The word "ascetic" arises in association with his sister's description of her husband. An image of a monk occurs to me, while the patient is describing his brother-in-law's law office and the man's inordinate preoccupation with his work. My patient is saying, "So I told him that he should now look after himself more carefully," but I am confused. Who is he referring to? The boy? The husband? It was not clear. The boy because he is postoperative—if this is indeed the right nephew (the patient has three)—or the sister's husband, who is suffering because of marital tensions? The confusion over who is being designated is woven into the preconscious tapestry of my patient's narrative and my own inner associations.

How does an analyst handle such confusion? Is he startled by this uncertain mental state? Does he reproach himself for failing to get details exactly right: *when* last week did the patient report that image? was it last week at all? perhaps it was only this Monday? Does he wonder whether the patient's communication represents unconscious dynamic *a* or unconscious dynamic *b*? Both are so plausible. He thinks of further possible dynamics: *c*, *d*, and *e*. And so it goes. Entertaining many ideas, the analyst's *frame of mind allies with the unconscious*, adopting a mentality that, as it becomes timeless, plastic, and open to contradiction, develops into an unconscious sensibility.

Sensibilitas, originally meaning the capacity for physical sensation, refers to an individual's "receptiveness to impression," a "capacity to respond perceptively to intellectual, moral, or aesthetic values," stressing "delicate, sensitive awareness or responsiveness." The OED links the word to feelings—"the power or faculty of feeling, capacity of sensations or emotion as distinguished from cognition or will"—and to "emotional consciousness." From a psychoanalytic perspective, sensibility refers to an individual's unconscious capacity to receive the object world, which results in more sensitive contact with the other and a greater reliance on feelings than on cognition. I return to this later but suggest here that sensibility is akin to what I have called a *separate sense*, that sense deriving from an unconsciousness increasingly devoted to communication. If we recall Freud's statement that unconscious communication is a form of psychic action, we can appreciate how this fits in with object-relational views of projective and introjective identification, which concern how one person acts upon the other and how the other's response (even if only intrapsychic) derives from the shape of the action. Knowing that the analyst has devolved his consciousness in favor of more associative and unconscious levels of functioning, the patient will preconsciously perceive that this particular sensibility is sensitive to the unconscious. As the patient puts both himself and his objects into the analyst's dreaming, he knows that he contributes to it, and uses the analyst as an important participant in his own increased unconsciousness, the prerequisite for analytical sensibility. He senses that he contributes to the analyst's dreaming, affecting the analyst's unconscious but not reaching his consciousness as such— so privacy is assured. Perhaps this is not unlike the dreaming person who knows he is inside a dream but does not challenge it, even to the point of assuming no dream is taking place. I wonder if this negative hallucination serves the patient's need to be unvigilant in order for the dreaming to take place, or rather, as Freud said, to preserve sleep, to which we may add: to preserve being.

Freud wrote that "the *Ucs.* is alive and capable of development" and "accessible to the impressions of life" (1915, 190). When the psychoanalyst devolves his consciousness, he creates a mood that analysands perceive, in a manner not dissimilar to the analyst's own perception of the patient's move into unconsciousness; and whatever the interpretative outcome of these twin recognitions, both participants are in fact *developing the unconscious*, creating a theater for its enactment, providing a safe place for its plays, and thereby increasing its effectiveness in the therapeutic process. This is precisely what happens when the analyst encourages the patient to free-associate and when he engages himself in evenly hovering attentiveness: the space is open for unconscious play. This idea of the function of unconscious development and unconscious communication challenges the view of Freud and the ego psychologists that analysis aims to render the unconscious conscious. In fact, both need each other to be meaningful. Free association, when the unconscious is given a free voice, is a liberating process in its own right. We devolve consciousness to heightened unconsciousness in order to experience our being, just as we sharpen our analytical objectifications to comprehend mental life and the nature of our idiom.

What does the analyst do after devolving consciousness in order to dream his patient? He works with counter-transference dreaming exactly as he would with a patient's dream; reflecting on the preceding material in the hour (equivalent to day residue), he creates links between the patient's discourse and his own unconscious redistribution of its manifest contents. This work expresses the continuous labor of preconscious linking, for the analyst will see that earlier parts of the hour now assume increased significance because they generated his own dream work.

Returning to the manifest material (narratives, moods, actions) presented by a patient is to move from deep experience back to shallow meanings, though shallow here does not mean less informative. The manifest narratives and actions serve as continuous points of retrospective reference for the analyst moving from countertransference dreaming to attentive listening and interpreting, not unlike the mental positioning he assumes when he hears a dream, associates, and reflects. When a patient tells me his dream about going to IKEA, it evokes an immediate set of associations for me: first I think of the word "key," then "I," and this sponsors an image—not immediately comprehensible—of my patient on a beach standing in the sun. Further associations occupy my more immediate thoughts while the patient continues to talk about what he did after going to IKEA. After my rather intense period of association, I recover to wonder what he then talked about, which I retrieve, since part of me was listening to him all along.

The analyst will give way to his own associations during the silences between concentrated and focused listening. He is also aware of a paradox: that his own interpretations call upon the patient's more focused consciousness and interrupt the patient's inner associative process; they might be, then, strangely antithetical to the creativity of unconscious processes. But the patient's associations to an interpretation break it up, and many analysts practicing today see this not as resistance to the hidden truth of the comment, but as an immediate unconscious use of the truth of the interpretation.

The analyst has other choices. He may decide against an interpretation proper and opt for comments more akin to association. I told the IKEA patient that the word "key" came to mind, as did the color yellow, the color of the IKEA building, associations which, when one looks back, could be seen to break up the manifest content of the dream and give voice to certain important hidden ideas carried by it. This kind of work appeals less to focalized consciousness and more to the collaboration of both participants, working unconsciously together.

When such an episode works, the analytical couple engage in a free-associative discourse that partly expresses the nature of unconscious thought itself; indeed, when Freud wrote of the relation between the unconscious and consciousness, he indicated that "the derivatives of the *Ucs.* . . . act as intermediaries between the two systems" and "open the way" to communication between them (1915, 194). The same holds true of those derivatives of the analyst's and the patient's unconscious when each is disclosing thoughts that are in the nature of free associations. The derivatives are the intermediaries, operating in a space that Winnicott was to designate "the intermediate area of experiencing": when he considered the nature of analytical work, he designated this as the area of play, following Freud's description of the transference scene as a "playground." The emphasis here is not on intentional play, but on the fact that play occurs whenever two people spend time together, think together, and speak to, act upon, and behave with each other.

Although the mother creates an illusion of unity with her infant, this illusion recedes during the late Oedipal period, when the child discovers that the complexity of his internal world and the shifting matrix of group life dissolve the simpler—and simplifying—psychic structures such as those built around the mother-infant relationship or the Oedipal triangle. Neither an affiliation with the matriarchal order nor identification with the patriarchal order will resolve this Oedipal recognition, when the child finds that his mind generates a complex world that defies cohering fables. Then latency inaugurates a lifelong creative retreat from this recognition: the child who realizes that mental life and group processes are too complex to be adequately thought has learned something, though he will also insist on his ignorance. As each person develops there is always this split between the wise self and the fooled self, the shrewd and the innocent.

It is interesting that psychoanalysis, which would have us look truth in the eye, also makes use of the most powerful illusion we generate: that we convey ourselves to other people. Sitting silently, "umming" along to sustain the illusion, the analyst supports the patient's belief that he understands everything, an illusion that encourages the patient's efforts. More specifically, the analyst does not repeatedly admit that he cannot comprehend much of what is being said to him; indeed, in spite of his knowledge of the counterfeit nature of unconscious representation, the analyst believes that he can and will understand his patient and indicates as much. By paraphrasing or repeatedly seeking a clarification the analyst informs the patient that he understands.

I wonder. Is the analyst wise because he realizes how comparatively little *can* be known? The notion of the shrewd censor preventing ideas from reaching consciousness may be wishful thinking. According to Freud, the internal censor had to be fooled by the work of the unconscious. With displacement, for example, something of the hidden idea tries to reach consciousness: e.g., fear of the father is experienced as fear of horses. However true the idea that we try to stop certain wishes and memories from entering consciousness, the idea of a constant battle with an exceptionally shrewd censor is just

as likely to be a wish for a companion to our unconscious. What if we do just think unconsciously? What if
we have turned our censor-self into an imaginary companion, giving our unconscious a dummy? If so, the analyst
uttering his traditional "um" plays the stooge rather well
with his dummy voice. A moment ago I argued that each
sustains an illusion of understanding. Now it seems to be
simply a game both play well.

In my view, the analyst plays both figures in the transference: the wise figure who sustains illusion and thereby
encourages the patient to speak, and the fool who does
not know what is being said to him. And analysands believe
their analysts (to a varying extent, of course) to be wise
fools, both all-knowing and ignorant. For however pertinent, lasting, comforting, and profound the analyst's
interpretative work, the patient also understands the use-
fulness but fragility of the analyst's dummy self, the one
who says "um" while being fooled by the patient's inner
experience. How could it be otherwise? As the patient
talks—a narrative over the course of the hour becomes a
free association—he has what we might call "back of the
mind" thoughts, parallel but less easily articulated associations not heard by the analyst. When the analyst senses
that a patient is hesitating because of these unspoken
thoughts, he may interrupt and inquire about these other
ideas. But though they may then be reported, no patient
can tell it all.

Both know this and accept that an illusion of understanding is essential to the creation of meaning. The
analyst will be affected by the patient's use of displacement,
condensation, and substitution. In the recurrent and intense displacements which feature in the transference, the

analyst is pushed into an image, a mood, a narrative place, or affected by parapraxes or the logic implicit in the sequence of any freely spoken ideas; his thoughts and feelings are derivatives of the patient's unconscious. But how can we differentiate between the analyst's elaboration of the patient's unconscious and his own idiomatic disseminations? We cannot. All we can do is recognize the difference between idioms—a recognition which assumes a kind of tensional authority and creates a boundary that fosters the freedom of unconscious play.

Often it is difference, not similarity, misunderstanding rather than understanding, that elicits unconscious communication. A patient mentions a backache in the early part of the hour, talks about hanging clothes in the cupboard, describes a dance the night before, and then says what I mistakenly hear as "So I bopped so much I [mumbled, inaudible] took out Shelley." I say: "Shelley?" He: "Who is that?" Me: "I thought you said that you took out Shelley." He (laughing): "No, I said that I took out my skeleton . . . hurt my spine." We pause. I admit my parapraxis was curious and wonder out loud why I thought of his skeleton as feminine—I imagined Shelley to be female—as if he were "hanging" around the spinal frame of a woman. As I say this an image of a coat hanger comes to mind and then he talks about how his friends have always teased him about his posture. Another silence. "Well, it's funny, you know, but my self image is of myself—as flesh—draped around my mother's body . . . it has been a recurring image of my body for most of my life." My mishearing distorted his manifest content and created an unconscious meaning that proved in this instance analytically fruitful.

If a patient has unconscious freedom, then his analyst will be spoken to, affected, characterized, expected, received, and resisted in a freewheeling manner that expresses not simply the nature of unconscious movement but, more precisely, the complex shape of the other's idiom of personality. Even if that idiom is too complex to be put into descriptive terms, we nonetheless have our own precise experience of it, such that we can feel within ourselves the difference between one person's idiom and another's.

To gain a clearer understanding of how we are affected by the organizing movement of the other, let us look at the opening of *Moby-Dick*.

Call me Ishmael. Some years ago—never mind how long precisely—having little or no money in my purse, and nothing particular to interest me on shore, I thought I would sail about a little and see the watery part of the world. (12)

The content here is fairly simple. The narrator tells us his name, says that sometime in the past, having little money and nothing special to engage his interest on the shore, he went to sea. But when we examine the specific means of telling us these contents, we are affected by his particular way of conveying his thoughts, and thus we are *in-formed* of his narrative idiom. "Call me Ishmael" brings us quite close rather roughly and brusquely. Quite specific, really—"Ishmael." Then he pushes us back—"never mind how long precisely"—as if we had inquired how long he had been away, which may not have crossed our mind. And he is vague. He does not say how many years ago he set sail. Anyway, why should it be a mystery. What does he mean by "little or no money"? Did he have any or not?

Of course, we can guess generally what he means, but it's the effect which is of interest—"little" or "no," to which I associate at this moment the concepts of being "little" and "no."

Certainly the way the words are arranged in relation to one another—their form—brings about the peculiar effect of this narrator. "I thought I would sail about a little": Where? On a pond? No, the oceans of the world. Again "little." The effect of an understatement. Also whimsical, but just after a brusque beginning. Finally, "and see the watery part of the world," which of course refers to the seas, but what a wonderfully odd way to put it! The effect upon myself? "Watery" feels to me like the ocean and is strangely childlike in its aptness. It also evokes associations to a woman's body—to the womb—but distinguishing this watery area as a "part" of the world evokes the earthly and the relation between the watery and the terrestrial.*

As Norman Holland (1973) has argued, no critic can divorce his reading from the peculiar effect of the text upon his identity, so there will be neither two identical readings of a text nor a final, correct one. Holland's work examines a type of unconscious work between the idiom of the author's text and the personality of the reader, in which it is not possible to distinguish between the actions of the text and the reader's response, so intertwined do they become.

Reading a text and being with an actual person, however, are quite different engagements, and the literary experience only serves as an example of something that takes place in more deeply complex and unconscious ways when

---

* For a different and yet more detailed response to the very same passage, see David Leverenz, "Moby Dick" (1970).

two people play upon each other's idiom. As I discuss below, illness in a person, like a theme in a text, is comparatively easy to find but is not equivalent to the idiom of either. It is important to keep this in mind when considering the nature of an individual's unconscious and his unconscious communication, because when it works it is beyond our consciousness: it is not the stuff of organized comment, but most profoundly the work of different forms of being. Melville's fictional idiom is not in the thematic contents of his novels but in his specific manner of writing: in the forming of the content.

Analogy with musical interpretation may further help to clarify this difference between form and content. A musical composition is a form in which musical notes are arranged in a very particular manner. As we hear it, each of us is processed by its particular logic. The experience of being processed by the music is perhaps more clearly grasped when we think of the differences in our subjective state brought about by different conductors' interpretations. Bernstein and Giulini both take a common object—let us say Mahler's Fifth Symphony—and each interprets it according to his own idiom, transforming the form, and as we listen to one or the other interpretation, we are moved by this common object in very different ways. Part of the pleasure of attending a concert is that although we may know the music quite well, we do not know how the conductor and orchestra will play it on that night, and each of us knows that we will be processed by at least two forms: the music itself and the intelligence conveyed by the conductor's interpretation of it.

When I listen to a patient describing his life, I of course note similarities with other patients. But even as he tells me a story which might elicit in my mind memories of other lives—and thus bring me to aspects of what people have in common—I am being put through a process that is the swift trace of his idiom. Being moved about by the patient, I respond by transforming his material into my own, unconsciously resignifying it according to my own unconscious processes. Just as I know the difference of form as interpretation through the hands of Bernstein or Giulini, so I know the difference in my patients through the way they conduct the analysis.

Naturally I am in possession of my own subjectivity. I will reconstruct what I hear from the other and my hearing will differ from that of any other listener. My history as a subject makes me full of my own mental contents. But each patient organizes my contents differently. Even as an unconscious subject I am still shaped by another's effect upon me. My self is given a new form by the other.*

If each patient is to be found in and through the analyst's countertransference—bearing in mind that (like many psychoanalysts) I broaden this term to include the analyst's theories and interpretations as well as his more unconscious responses—are we to conclude that there is no object available to him which is the outcome of the patient's and analyst's work together? This brings us to different terrain, which I have discussed in *Being a Character*, where I argued that the analytical couple unconsciously specify an area of work to which they both contribute and where eventually the analysand develops a new psychic structure. I term this a "psychic genera" to

---

* I establish an internal object that bears the proper name of another person, and when I think of that person, this object is released to its own experiencing. Although preconscious and conscious objectifications of the other contribute to this formation of an internal object, it is an internal structure, constructed unconsciously.

indicate its generative function, insofar as the newly developed psychic structure offers wide new perspectives on the world of objects and upon the self.

As the analyst listens to the patient's discourse, much of what he hears does not make sense until the patient supplies something new that retrospectively confers sense upon the chaos. In "Recommendations," Freud hints that this moment may take a long time to arrive: "The undeserved compliment of having 'a remarkably good memory' which the patient pays one when one reproduces some detail after a year and a day can then be accepted with a smile, whereas a conscious determination to recollect the point would probably have resulted in failure" (112–13). The smile is surely a sign of the analyst's pleasure at having gained access to the patient's unconscious by abandoning the self to all thoughts that cross his mind: weeks, months, even "a year and a day" go by before the chaos becomes clear and the analyst may bring forth a coherent interpretation.

Despite the fact that both patient and psychoanalyst know that only a meager part of unconscious mental life is knowable, they are nevertheless driven to search for this knowledge. As each struggles to understand an unconscious development, or when one participant has an inspired grasp of previously unconscious feelings, their mutual effort is honored and rewarded. We must therefore acknowledge those unconscious communications of unconscious contents that do reach consciousness in a psychoanalysis. Even if they are the exception to the rule, the analyst is required to use his training and expertise to decipher them, and it is they that the analysand brings for treatment. To what do I refer?

A patient repeats traumatic experiences which give no

pleasure and are simply authorized by his neurotic need, amounting to a kind of urge, to repeat the disturbance. Psychoanalysts are well aware of the pathological structures their patients repeat in the transference. The very nature of repetition demonstrates the foreclosure of the unconscious (its elaborative and derivative movement) and eventually makes it possible for the analyst to understand and fully analyze a complex unconscious content. Illness restricts freedom. Whether it is the analysand's symptom or pathological character structure, illness allows for perhaps the most salient unconscious mental contents to be communicated and worked on through interpretation. Although the intrinsically therapeutic analytical relation is important here, and although the analyst's holding function significantly contributes to the patient's cure, it is in and through his interpretative work, repeated again and again, that he opposes and deconstructs the pathological structures.

By examining the symptom or the pathological structure we learn more about the nature of unconscious life, which becomes intriguing if we consider that the illness itself may transmit the patient's inner unconscious contents to the other. Does transmitting the illness become a way to convey unconscious contents?

When Freud reached his understanding of this form of communication, he conceptualized his theory of the death instinct. There was something beyond pleasure that could be in the service either of life (i.e., procreative) or of death (as in repeatedly self-destructive behavior). Even though Freud was obliged to discuss the life instinct at this point in his theory, it was his discovery of the death instinct that was so compelling: the patient could live out a self-destructive pattern that conscripted all forms of desire into the armies of negation. Death work can destroy the unconsciousness of the unconscious.

Although illness restricts freedom, this does not mean that an unconscious free to work its contents will process only benign ideas: it is important to differentiate a healthy process—here, the dream work of the unconscious—from its contents, which may be quite disturbed. To say that unconscious freedom is important to mental well-being is not to include the contents the unconscious is processing, and the psychoanalyst, while appreciating the vigor of an unconscious process, will usually be aware that certain specific ideas being developed are in themselves indications of considerable conflict which must be analyzed.

As we shall see in the next chapter, unconscious communication between two people is not necessarily about constructing lucid, effective, and memorable understandings of one another; rather, it is a way of life—for people in fairly constant proximity to one another. One person's direct effect on the other—unconscious to unconscious—cannot be witnessed by consciousness. It is a discordant symphonic movement of a reciprocally infinite falling of one self into another. There are harmonic duets, that is for sure: two people sharing mental processes and ills. But the effect of one person upon another is ordinarily too idiosyncratic to be comprehended.

The tenuous hold of consciousness upon the unconscious does not, in my view, mean that we must take the pessimistic view that analytical work is outside consciousness. It may seem strange to honor work that occurs beyond the intentional influence of the analyst's understanding, but the process works, and as time passes in a psychoanalysis the analyst has increased regard for a methodology of which he is only a part. The process of free association not only establishes a mood suited to unconscious communication; its (often lengthy) silences become birthplaces of important emotional realities for both participants. The terms we use for emotions—anxiety, depression, love, or hate—are desperately inadequate, but it is fitting that they should be so clumsy, because when we share an emotional reality, it is as if unconscious communication takes place by means of our separate senses, communication devoted to knowings derived from feelings.

When the psychoanalyst enters the special frame of mind which I have termed evenly hovering attentiveness, and when he invites the patient to associate freely, he creates the connection between his own unconscious and that of his patient. He opens the door to their unconscious communications and makes possible a highly special form of work that, while beyond their conscious control, gives a psychoanalysis its uniquely creative force.

2

A Separate Sense

Conversing with a friend I say, "Let's go to hear the Birmingham Symphony Orchestra's concert next week, as I quite like their conductor, er . . ." and my friend says, "Simon Rattle," effortlessly finishing my sentence. A patient is telling me about a colleague with whom he has been having a hard time: "I know this man is a bully, and I can cope with his insensitivities, but that is not the point. I find that I feel something else, a sense that I am . . . ," at which point I say "inadequate," and the patient answers in the affirmative with great relief.

Now, how did I know to say "inadequate"? I could as easily have said "angry," "despairing," "a wimp." But I am able to intuit the missing word. Magic? Not if we see this type of forgetting, on the part of the first person, and remembering on the part of the second, as a subtle elisionary act that enhances unconscious communication. And not if, in psychoanalysis, we recognize the intelligence behind the patient's continuous creation of such elisionary moments. Over time, as the analyst fills in the gaps with the right words, the patient unconsciously in-forms the analyst's unconscious sensibility, which elicits signifers that utter his thoughts or feelings. Through this type of play, the analytical couple creates thousands of potential spaces, maximizing and deepening unconscious communications.

Although the analyst may sometimes speak the missing word or words, more often they remain unspoken. The more common fillings-in occur in the mind of both participants, who speak subvocally in a silent and free-moving inner dialogue, providing through the matches and mis-matches a rich discourse for their encounter. A patient says, "Last night I went to . . ." and I silently speak "the opera" but the patient says "the cinema." A patient says, "I am really very . . ."; I silently reply "cross," and the patient says "pleased with my work on the book." Each analyst engages in thousands of such responses and feels the course of the patient's correction, which gives him an unconscious sense of the patient's way of thinking. It is like learning a new language and may take years.

As the analysand's object, the analyst is continuously learning about aspects of the patient's psychic logic, intu-itively following some but not all of the patient's discourse and filling in gaps where sentences are left unfinished. In doing so, the analyst is focusing on certain unconscious ideas deployed by the patient. Together, they uncon-sciously designate areas to be investigated which in turn become psychic gravities that eventually form themselves into new ideas offering fresh perspectives (on the patient).

The elisionary action is an important part of the daily act of "reception," supplying the other with projected contents of the self. In some respects it is an ordinary form of the uncanny, of one person speaking the other's mind and the recipient not having to ask, "How did you know what I was going to say?" because this is assumed to be an ordinary part of relational knowing. The momentarily deleted word may be quickly discernible, such as "President François . . ." where "Mitterrand" easily fills the space, but psychoanalysis offers two people the opportunity to collaborate in a deeply unconscious way, creating profound caesurae that "find" the contents of the unconscious.

There are, as we know, other types of uncanny experience.

A psychoanalyst who had worked some two years before in an inner-city ghetto found himself in the neighborhood and decided to visit his old clinic. As he pulled into the parking lot, he remembered one of his favorite patients, a particularly beautiful woman who had a certain courage and integrity and hope that had enlivened the otherwise dreary atmosphere. A few minutes after his arrival he picked up the phone to call his secretary and was rather intensely involved in discussion when to his astonishment the clinic secretary informed him that the very woman he had been thinking about was on another line. He took the call, said hello and asked if she could call back in thirty minutes, which unfortunately—but aptly—she did not. The woman had not called the clinic for some two years. To the analyst it seemed uncanny that he should drive to the clinic and that this patient should call not only on the same day but during the same minutes.

A married couple are driving in their car, and having finished conversing briefly, they are now pleasantly lost in thought. Unbeknownst to each, they "happen" to be thinking of the same person whom they met some fifteen months before at a party but have not seen since. As the husband says, "You know, I've been thinking about . . . ," the wife quite spontaneously says "Ted." The husband rightly wonders how his wife could possibly know that he has been thinking about Ted, and the wife is stunned that she *knew* he had been thinking about Ted. The realization that she is not in the habit of doing this seems to rather weaken the "hit and miss" theory. Both are impressed by the arrival of the uncanny.

Freud describes a rather different experience in his essay "The Uncanny" (1919). While walking through a small Italian village on a hot day, he discovered much to his surprise that, on three occasions, each route he took led back to the very same street, one occupied by "painted women . . . seen at the windows of the small houses." Freud "hastened to leave the narrow street at the next turning" but return he did. Surprisingly enough, he does not analyze what seems rather obvious, that these apparently repellent women were in fact rather desirable, and his repetition compulsion may hardly have been beyond the pleasure principle. After all, he returns *three times* to the scene of the painted women—the number which signifies the Oedipal triangle.

This essay is a wonderfully complex piece of writing, both confusing and illuminating. Freud does not know what to make of the subject he has chosen. He begins by deconstructing the words *unheimlich* (unhomely), and *heimlich* (homely), arguing that the uncanny is ultimately an experience of being in an unhomely place, a place of fear, but by implication a fear that takes on meaning only in terms of its relation to the familiar. Musing on Schelling's statement that " '*unheimlich*' is the name for everything that ought to have remained . . . secret and hidden but has come to light" (224), he maintains that *unheimlich* is an intrinsic part of *heimlich*—opposites—so that the familiar always bears the unfamiliar in it.

He then misreads Hoffmann's tale "The Sand-Man" as

a true representation of the uncanny. In truth, the story bears little relation to uncanny experience; it is, rather, a tale of madness and a commentary on the literature of the double. Freud, though, follows an interesting line of association by proceeding to discuss Rank's work on the double. Then, intriguingly, he returns to discussing how the feelings of repetition repeat the dreamer's sense of helplessness. "I have observed . . . this phenomenon does undoubtedly, subject to certain conditions and combined with certain circumstances, arouse an uncanny feeling, which, furthermore, recalls the sense of helplessness experienced in some dream-states" (237). It is at this point in his essay that Freud describes his trip to the Italian village.

What might Freud be gaining by bringing up the hidden mystery, the sand-man, the double, and now the dream experience? What, we might ask, would fulfill this résumé? Would it not be that other side of us which is the unconscious ego, the ego that forms our experience, that is the intelligence behind the construction of the dream? We do not customarily see this part of us: it would appear to be impossible. The audience at a play does not see the production team behind the scenes; they witness only the actors on the stage, who enact the play. The dreaming subject inside the dream does not see the figure who dreams the dream—even though its wise processional presence is everywhere.

Let us return to the analyst making his visit to the clinic. Psychoanalysts know only too well the "anniversary response": a year after a significant event, a person will indicate a memory of that moment by unconsciously doing something to indicate the memory. The enactment takes the place of a memory which he is certainly inside, but, as in the dream, he appears oblivious to its meaning. So, for example, a man who heard of his father's illness on November 12 has since "forgotten" the significance of that distressing day, but one year later on November 12 he rents a video of a film in which a son must deal with the traumatic news of his father's illness. Perhaps action begets insight. Perhaps a friend reminds him. Or maybe his analyst asks him what he was doing on that day last year. When the link is made, the man is taken by his ability to stage and be staged by something uncanny.

The anniversary response suggests an extraordinary range of "timings" from the unconscious. The examples above are of synchronic memories, which repeat in time. In my own case an incident that occurred when I was nine was particularly traumatic, so the number 9 has a special unconscious meaning to me; and in 1969, 1979, and finally 1989 I was immersed in disturbing rememberings of this early trauma. It was only with the third repetition that I realized the special significance of 9. Indeed, it would be intriguing to have a "psychic calendar" which marked the days of each month which held a particular unconscious meaning for the individual. So much is either repressed or amnesically consigned, that the self may experience these subtle anniversaries as informed emotional moments contributing to the psychic intensities of everyday life.

So for the psychoanalyst visiting the clinic, it seems possible that he had developed, along with his patient, a certain sense of their time, so that when he thought of recontacting the clinic he did so in harmony with his patient, who also on that very day thought of the clinic. It was not telepathy that brought them together. It was simply, by chance, that on this day their unconscious sense of mutual timing was at work and expressed itself in this manner; in other words, it was time for these two people to think about each other, just as the anniversary response is the time for thinking about what it recalls. The husband and wife who are astonished to find themselves thinking of Ted at the very same moment will not know why they did so; presuming they exhaust obvious content ante-cedents—discussion of another Ted or of anyone con-nected to Ted—they will give up the search, because they cannot observe their own sense of mutually negotiated timings, nor would they ever know why they joined together over Ted and not over another mental content at that moment. It was simply time to think about Ted.

Freud astutely likened this situation to the helplessness of being in a dream, or returning to the mother's body, an intelligent free-narrative association as the mother and the neonate develop their own sense of mutual time. Later the infant informs the mother of his own time sense: when to be fed, when to be held, when to be rocked, when to rest, when to wake up. Later the child's moods inform the mother of the time she may relax, the time she can be usefully anxious, the time when she can safely express hate toward the child, the time when expressions of anger are not at all proper, the time when the child's fatigue is early malingering, the time when the child's tiredness is true exhaustion, the time for humor, the time for seri-ousness, the time for empathy, the time for confrontation, the time for intellection, the time for feelings, the time for being idealized, the time for being realized . . . the time for . . . : these times are the times of time in human relations, out of which the parent develops his or her separate sense of the child's time—a time sense not thought out, although not thoughtless, which operates at the level of the parent's unconscious ego as he or she is instructed by the child's timing of the self. Of course, this is a less than perfect temporal harmony. Each will be "out of synch," but such everyday errors or mistimings only verify the significance of the time sense as a factor in unconscious communication between two people.

———

A psychoanalyst develops a separate sense for each patient, attuned to the analysand's precise intelligence of form, as the patient takes the analyst through a process that derives entirely from the patient's aesthetic in being. The patient educates the analyst's sensibility, moving him along logical pathways that the analyst now knows are ideological positions. The analyst comes to sense the basic assumptions peculiar to the analysand's being, out of which he develops a sense of his patient's idiom.

But this separate sense is a universal potential, by no means restricted to the analytical relationship, although psychoanalysis exploits it to positive effect. I believe that our ordinary experiences of psychically intense moments during the day suggest to us the presence of unconscious meaning and unconscious work. We are preconsciously aware that such moments—the birthplaces of inspiration and reflection—will eventually prove meaningful: thus, during the day our separate sense makes us aware of this meaning, even if we have to wait for a fragmentary reflection on the day, or for the dream that will follow that night, or weeks, months, and even years hence before it will yield up something of its truth.

Yesterday, for example, I felt I "had" to look once again at a book on Dali's paintings, particularly paintings of his father. So I did this. Some hours later, I was in a restaurant talking with a friend about fathers and fathering, when the feeling I had during the day was echoed, only this time I thought of the elderly Americans who had come to England on a Liberty ship to take part in the D-Day celebrations. The moment passed. This morning I had a sudden idea that seemed to be part of the dissemination of this strand of feelings of the day before. I thought of returning once again to see the Dali exhibit because I felt I had not taken enough time to study his transition from Cubist-type paintings to Surrealism proper. This gave rise to a hypothesis that Surrealism expresses a necessary violence against the patriarchal order. One can see in the chain of my associations the significance of the father, the notion of returning to the father, the concept of not having had enough time to see an important transition, and further themes implicit in my interest in the D-Day celebrations and in the liberation this important day stood for. At the time of experiencing these intensities, however, I did not know what they meant. I only followed my sense of an inner significance. I felt I was at work on some new understanding—for myself—of recent lived experience. We follow these paths every day of our lives, and they are evidence of that undramatic, indeed quite ordinary, creativity of unconscious processes.

The sense is the thing. Not the particular contents it reveals, especially in a psychoanalysis, because much of the time these thoughts will consist of the analyst's own deeply private inner associations which hardly link to what the patient is saying. But the analyst will inevitably choose which of the patient's disseminations to follow, and in so doing make crucial decisions about the outcome of that week's or month's work. A psychoanalyst may mistakenly select less significant valorizations over more important disseminations and therefore waste substantial amounts of the patient's time. The analyst's *introjection* of the patient's idiom (when he is used as an object), then, develops a shadow ego which is crucial to the clinician's ability to create a separate sense for his patient.

Bion (1965) wrote extensively about the function of intuition in psychoanalysis. He saw analyst and analysand as sharing an emotional experience which, if indefinable, comes as close to an absolute truth in the analytic hour as anything will; he assigns to such a truth an arbitrary letter, O, to stand for the thing in itself. To get to the truth the analyst must allow himself to become one with O, to submit to the emotional experience of the session, which can only be accomplished if he dispenses with memory (of previous sessions) and desire (to accomplish something). Emotional experience—which Bion fails to define—is the basis of intuition. According to him, the intuitive sense derives from the emotional experience. It is from "there," inside such experience, that one gains intuitive ability. In his view, the psychoanalysts' special training in intuition applicable to the psychoanalytical situation enables them to "see" psychological phenomena that nonanalysts cannot.

If we assume that such a separate sense exists, just how does it work? Working with a patient, an analyst comes to develop an inner constellation of preconscious ideas, feelings, visual images, sonic metaphors, somatic dispositions, and body-ego acuities, a kind of psychosomatic organization that forms his matrix for unconscious communication with his patient. This separate intuitive sense is a network of the many different planes of reference that constitute subjectivity. Each register of lived experience generates its own type of significance, and they all work simultaneously to form subjectivity. Lacan's view of the self in pieces (*corps morcelé*) and Klein's view of the self as continuously staging a paranoid-schizoid position are efforts to identify phenomenologically a complexity that knows no unity; indeed, the place of the subject is the intersection of forces that, *taken together*, constitute a continuous questioning of one's being. The "body in pieces" or the "paranoid-schizoid" world are simply metaphors of subjectivity itself, and the Lacanian and Kleinian cures—however intriguing and worthy—oversimplify a fact that will not vanish with the ideology of progression toward a curative point, whether depressive or linguistic.

Each school of psychoanalysis aims to establish its own guidelines for effective clinical work, rules which the analysand in training experiences as a patient, discusses in the supervisory relationship, and then renegotiates with each and every one of his own patients whom he treats. It is important, however, to bear in mind that any good technique is an operational intelligence, as the analyst puts into effect what he believes to be the best psychoanalytic intervention.

The technique practiced by a psychoanalyst implicitly recognizes the dense, moving complexity that is the patient's fragmenting elaboration of idiom. Ego psychologists in particular identified the essentials of technique with the psychology of form: what do you pick out of the material to emphasize, in what manner, in what time frame, and with what task in mind? Decisions about how to discuss something with a patient are inevitably guided by what the analyst terms "clinical judgment," which here we may understand to be his unconscious sense of timing and his intuitive sense of what is of predominant "interest" to the patient.

Analytical "craftsmanship" reveals an "operational intelligence." How matters are handled is crucial. This unconscious sense of what the other needs ultimately derives from that kind of unconscious intuition that typifies the operational intelligence of early maternal and paternal care: rules for proceeding often based not on carefully thought-out actions in a session but on an unconscious sense of the correctness of a given intervention.

The analyst's technique joins with the analytical procedure to create a condition that calls up the patient's earliest relations to the object world. Over time both participants establish a sense of the other as process, which creates a sense of time shared by the two: a time for the patient and the analyst to talk about the mother, a time to discuss the father, a time for the discussion of sexuality, a time for the full discussion of guilt, a time for remembering the traumas from the real, a time for scrutiny of secondary gain from such traumas, a time for the deconstruction of fantasy, a time for . . . Patient and analyst develop their own time together and, out of it, a certain unconscious communication of when it is time to discuss a particular issue.

The analyst's technique shows his unconscious collaboration with the patient's unconscious communications, and inevitably we must turn to the aesthetics of form—the particular way something is conveyed—as an important feature of unconscious communication. Unfortunately Freud was less than interested in the specific formal intelligence—or aesthetic—of any person's ego, so little that even though creating a dream is an aesthetic action, Freud preferred to see it solely as one of necessity.

Freud's reluctance to create a theory of unconscious form is all the more puzzling given that Schiller, whom he read and whose work he admired, had made a very great deal of the aesthetics of form. In his *Letters*, Schiller distinguishes between the individual's personality (*Persön-*

lichkeit), or self (*Selbst*), and his condition (*Zustand*). A person has determining attributes which persist throughout life; personality is a determinant form. But, of course, one's conditions change and alter one's being; life's "material of activity" (*Materie der Tätigkeit*) is received by the person but also changed by his personality in a never-ending mutuality of influence: "Only inasmuch as he changes does man exist; only inasmuch as he remains unchangeable does he exist" (75). Considered by itself, personality, according to Schiller, "is merely the predisposition to a possible expression of his infinite nature," a view that Winnicott was to hold of the true self. He would have also no doubt agreed with Schiller's linking of personality to the environment: "as long as he has neither perceptions nor sensations, he is nothing but form and empty potential." In order for the individual to come into his being, "he must impart form to matter; in order not to be mere form, he must give reality to the predisposition he carries within him," or "externalize all that is within him, and give form to all that is outside him" (77). Indeed there is a specific urge to give form to one's lived experiences, in Schiller's view, a form drive (*Formtrieb*).

If we understand this form drive to be the ego's desire to express the intelligent process of living, it is certainly missing in Freud's theory of the unconscious. Had Freud attended more closely to Schiller's writing (and it is an intriguing mystery why he did not), he could easily have followed Schiller's distinction between the "sense drive," the "form drive," and the "play drive," finding in the sense drive the elements of instinctual life, and in the form drive that peculiar organization of intelligence that is the individual's ego. It is that part of the unconscious which befuddled Freud in *The Ego and the Id*—the unconscious that is not part of the repressed but part of the machinery of repression. He could not see that he was merely dealing with the difference between content and form: the repressed unconscious refers to mental contents banished from consciousness, while the process of repression refers to an intelligence of operation that reveals the individual's personality as it transforms the contents of lived experience.

The eros of form is the pleasure of creation. Instinctual urges and libido are an important part of the erotics of self, but we would now have to see the instincts as part of the drive to create. The so-called component instincts—of parts of the body such as the mouth, anus, and genitals—have their own mental representations, but the erotic drive is to find expression for such urges. In my view, Freud stated this very clearly in his model of the progression of the instinct from its somatic source to its aim, which is to be discharged in the creation of an object—an activity that is a formal procedure for managing the instinctual drives. The aim of sexual urges is not simply bodily gratification, important as that is; in my view, the desire to populate the inner world with excitements and objects of desire is as significant, and gives form to the component instincts that ultimately express the movement of the total personality through the object world.

The particular way that an individual gives form to his lived experiences, the way he constructs his internal and external worlds, involves unconscious communication as aesthetic. To shape one's form out of a matrix of potentially infinite somethings is in itself deeply pleasurable. It is interesting that the word "idiom" derives from the Greek verb *idio-ome*, which is the same root as the one for the word "id," and although the etymology is complex, the concept of form—specifically to form through incorporation—is one aspect of the word's meaning. To shape—to re-present—is perhaps not just a pleasure but a demand. So returning to Freud with this in mind, I think we could say that his concept of the id—which never gained purchase in French psychoanalysis, was dropped by ego psychologists, and has never been favored by object-relations theorists or American relational thinkers—was inadequately conceptualized in the first place. Freud was right to think of this "x" as the foundation of the self from which a part (the ego) eventually emerged to deal with reality. But by making the id conceptually over-determined—on the one hand, it was a seething cauldron of primitive urges seeking discharge in any manner, and on the other, an intelligence of form which could develop—Freud joined form and content in a conceptual muddle that eventually spelled the end of an important idea. Winnicott rethought the id without saying so, terming it the "true self" and rightly situating it somewhere between the id and the ego of the structural model. I find "idiom" a more precise concept, insofar as it specifies the dense particularity of personality. The words "idiom" and "id" share the same root, and we may consider such particularity of individual form to be a specific entity which like a seed is endowed with the blueprint for its destiny—influenced in its journey by the very specific events and persons in its life.

Expression of one's idiom, therefore, quietly develops that aspect of the separate sense that pertains to the aesthetics of a life rather than the specific mental contents of one's existence. Each person's way of conveying his or her inner experiences reflects unconscious formings as unique and special as a novelist's, when the novel shows us familiar situations but rendered so differently as to make each representation unique and new. Analysts listening to their patients, and then deciding what to say and how to say it, do so substantially unconsciously, and their decision about how to put something, and its ultimate form of expression, are unconsciously linked to the analysand's receptive intelligence. In a good working alliance between analyst and patient, the former learns how to put things to the latter so that the communication reaches the patient in the most efficacious form possible. This intelligence is an important part of intuiting the other—a way of feeling the other out by forming and transforming contents until one develops a genre specific to the patient.

This is nowhere more visible than in the psychoanalytic treatment of a developmentally deprived person, one who has not received adequate understanding from a mother or a father. Although analysis of his inner life is, of course, very important to such a patient, so too is the act of forming and transforming his ideas and feelings into words, perhaps for the first time. Again, this process is largely unconscious, and partly derived from listening to the patient. The separate sense—that skill that derives from unconscious ability and unconscious communication—comes in large part from the exercise of the style of self and the idiom of each other's in-forming of one another. This in-forming is pleasing. Free association, when both participants are engaged in a mutually informative exchange, is a specific pleasure of psychoanalysis as it exercises the aesthetic functions of both patient and analyst.

Although analysts of most schools are quick to point out how frustrating and painful the analytical process is, they shy away from describing its deep pleasure. After all, how can this pleasure be justified? Better to emphasize the abstinence, the frustration, the pain, the travails, the pathologies, the resistances, the negative transferences, than to reveal the pleasure that is the source, the aim, and the gratified object of psychoanalysis. And as to cure? That pleasure should be a means of cure? That the free-associative process which gratifies the analysand's urges to express the self should be the essential means of transformation from pathology to well-being, that the analyst's technique should be his pleasure in the handling of the patient, that two people in such a place should acknowledge such a pleasure: this seems as yet an impossibility. Freud predicted that human sexuality would be the first casualty of the passage of time as resistance to the realization of our urges would demand their repression and their displacement. How uncanny that he himself would repress the sexual gratification of the very process he invented, stressing its travails and its abstinence, and thus exiling it from his theory. The pleasure of analysis is not to be found in the theories of psychoanalysis, except under the Presbyterian scowls of "actings-in" or "actings-out." As with Freud, so now with contemporary psychoanalysis, it is left to the patients furtively to tell friends how much fun a week of analysis has been, often when it has been very distressing. Freud's analysands' accounts of their work with him hardly describe joyless occasions. They write of its pleasure in a gossipy voice. Perhaps this is a fitting place for the greatest of pleasures: the love of re-presentation.

When the psychoanalyst and his patient are in unconscious communication with one another during those often mutually silenced spaces between them, they are each engaged in increasingly familiar found reveries to which both give substantial amounts of time. Even though each will have only a fractional conscious understanding of the other at any one time, both are nonetheless deeply involved with each other, and although unconscious communication is by definition out of sight and outside of consciousness, any well-functioning analytical couple would say that paradoxically what they cannot bring into consciousness about their collaboration—that which is always unconscious—is the deepest matrix of their work together. They are, as I have argued, exercising a separate sense that reaches through the barriers exercised by the limits of consciousness. This form of knowing and being known is profoundly pleasurable. It is blissful to free-associate in the sentient presence of the other who listens without making demands. To be received is to find something in the other that will receive the precise movements of one's own unconscious life.

That a psychoanalysis should be so gratifying is not a surprise. That its theoreticians should shudder from this fact is a curious oblation of the pleasures of unconscious communication.

3

Dissemination

Everyday experiences evoke what Freud called "psychic intensities," as a slightly different "degree of interest" arises in a single moment that awakens memories, instinctual states, and vivid thoughts. Such psychic intensities become "latent thoughts," congregations of unconscious views of experience transformed from what Bion termed *Beta elements*—undigested and meaningless facts of existence—to *Alpha elements*, mental material stored for dreams and thoughts to come. Something in what the French call *le vécu* (the lived experience) has had a very particular *psychic* effect, and records itself as a constellation of the self's experience at that very moment. For overdetermined reasons a single moment in a day becomes more intense than previous moments, because something has happened within the unconscious to create meaning.

Because a latent thought is an unconscious idea, it differs from the way the conscious mind, with its discretionary powers of judgment, rationally bifurcates lived experience. It is laden with psychic material that consciousness knows to be crucial to its own development: the stuff of somatic registrations, bodily recollections or dispositions, instinctual excitations, sensed memories of previously lived experience, elicited laws of being and relating that have been part of the individual's history, object-relational evocations in which specific unconscious relations to persons in one's past life are brought partly into being again, and so on.

A psychic intensity is also something of a questioning, when the individual implicitly asks what has happened, but in doing so unleashes the dispersing forms of the question itself. Thus a latent thought is not only a complex statement of one's immediate being but also a questioning of that being, and, as Freud realized, through discovering free association, any condensation simply raises a plenitude of questions.

What happens to latent thoughts accruing from these psychic intensities? As the person moves into sleep, newly formulated latent thoughts compete for dream representation. Excitedly questioned by the thoughts of the day, the person needs to be unburdened of the excitation in order to sleep in peace; the dream discharges the excitement, but not the meaning, by creating false answers in order to ensure sleep, and yet it preserves the deep meanings of a day's questionings. How does it do this?

By further condensation. Imagine that on my way to the library I pass a record store and see in the window an advertisement for Philip Glass's opera *Akhenaten*. I am unsure whether to go into the store or not, as it may be a waste of my time. I delay a few moments. I walk to the door, but I hesitate: I think of the library and the work to be done. On impulse I plunge into the store. As I look at the record, I think of when I saw the opera and all that "went into" that evening. But what went into that evening cannot be thought as such: it is more a dynamic inner constellation of experience in itself, the feelings, images, and inner sounds I remember are only partial representations of that episode.

I also think of my son, who first encountered "history" by studying Egypt, and how he made a papier-mâché Nile and countryside of an Egyptian kingdom. I wonder if it was Akhenaten's? I know that he and I talked about Akhenaten when he was about five. "Inside" that recollection are divergent and endless subsidiary memories and dynamic constellations that seem to radiate out in many directions. I think about the story of Akhenaten, understood to be a precursor, if not the origin, of the Oedipus myth. I think about a friend of mine whose brother-in-law plays for Philip Glass, and as this thought arises, I drift off, imagining my friend and her life. I wonder if I really like minimalist music. John Cage's essays on silence cross my mind. I think in the flash of a second about silence before this line of thought dives through the name of Nina Coltart to Susan Sontag and fragments into a multitude of new lines of inquiry moving now *into* the unconscious. Minutes later, thinking about wishing, I intersect Nina Coltart again, as the image of her house and the name of her street, Well Road, crosses my mind, to submerge yet again as a new idea displaces it. At the record store, I hear some of Glass's music in my mind. Sounds good enough. I buy the record.

Then I go to the library to read up on the analytical literature on "confidentiality," but I find it dull and more or less gloss over the reading. I head home on the Underground, only to discover that I cannot find my glasses. I search for them in one pocket, then the next, to no avail. I imagine asking my wife if she would mind stopping off on her way to work to order me a new pair. I daydream this dialogue with my wife and the daydreaming goes off on a tangent. At my stop, I leave the carriage, and on the way upstairs, to give the Underground lady my ticket, I find my glasses. But where is my ticket? Another search. Then I find it, and hand it over to her. A hearty Jamaican, she exclaims, "My gosh, man, do things one at a time!" I laugh, feel a bit embarrassed, believe she has somehow uncannily known something about me, but how did she see it? An image endures of this woman, sitting on her chair: a rather handsome, middle-aged figure, with a curvaceous bottom that was wonderful to see.

I could go on, but the point I wish to make would only get lost in the complexity of ordinary life, even if the irony might be more to the heart of the matter. Let me ask a Freudian question. How do these psychic intensities—the record store, the library, the Underground ride, the encounter with the ticket lady—with all of their latent thoughts get into the dream that night? Perhaps through a single image: that of a glass. In the dream I might only see a glass, but that object will bear within it not only the organizations of those psychic intensities described above but all their tributaries of thought. Glass of course links to Philip Glass. Glossing over the literature comes into the image of a glass. The loss of my glasses. The woman who sees something about me and my love of her body. Each dream condenses differing psychic intensities into single images which discharge the subject of the day's excitements, but perhaps due to the exchange from excitation to representation, the dream imagery seems unduly vivid and intense. And so it should be! Each image carries so much.

What next? The dreamer is awakened by the day and may recall the dream event, even though it is now a most curious relation. I like the way Blanchot (1971) puts it:

Between the person who is sleeping and the person who is the subject of dream events, there is a fissure, a hint of an interval, a difference in structure; clearly it's not someone else, an entirely different person, but what exactly is it? And if, upon waking, we hastily and greedily take possession of the night's adventures as if they belonged to us, do we not do so with a certain sense of usurpation (as well as gratitude), do we not carry with us the memory of an irreducible distance, a peculiar sort of distance, a distance between self and self, but also a distance between all the characters and the various identities (however certain) we confer on them, a distance without distance, illuminating and fascinating, somewhat like nearing the far-off or making contact with remoteness? (xxi)

Freud's invention of the psychoanalytical process, however, creates an intriguing confusion between the two selves. He asks the dreamer to associate freely to specific images of the dream, and as the analysand does so he unwittingly experiences the cracking up of his narrative intention and the structure of his text: in the process of talking about the dream, its latent thoughts emerge through what Freud calls a process of "radiation." When the dreamer tries to get back to the dream, he is driven off by countless "trains of thought" that lead him in a multitude of directions. The dream report, then, puts the dreamer in an intermediate space, between the dense vividness of the actual dream experience and the remote memory of the dream the following day.

Unconscious mental life operates according to an oscillation that ensures its continuous—indeed ceaseless—function, as on the one hand unconscious work brings together through condensation otherwise disparate ideas, and on the other hand the process of free association then deconstructs these condensations. When Freud asked the analysand to free-associate to the dream, he frequently stressed that in so doing the patient dispersed the manifest content of the dream. What was created as an act of condensation—the dream event—is destroyed by the work of free association. Both processes, however—bringing together and cracking up—are important features of the unconscious and constitute its dialectic; each time a condensation is created, its saturation with meaning guarantees that it will break up in subsequent moments of elaboration, and each unit of meaning, compacted in the condensation, now follows its own destiny.

Free association is creative destruction. An overdetermined phenomenon—dream text or psychic intensity—is bursting with many ideas that break up into differing meanings *upon* free association. It is essential to one's personal freedom to break up lucid unities of thought, lest consciousness become a form of ideational incarceration. Indeed, the more profound a psychic intensity, the less permanent its registration in consciousness, for the ideas deriving immediately from it soon give birth to a plenitude of further and divergent thoughts which disseminate in countless ways.

Freud, of course, followed differing trains of thought to find points of convergence in order to interpret "the meaning of the dream," and those who read *The Interpretation of Dreams* cannot but be impressed by his inventiveness, but also by a contradiction. As he indicated, no dream can be fully interpreted—it contains too many truths—and as psychoanalysts well know, certain dreams reported by analysands return again and again within the course of an analysis for "new considerations," which do not eradicate the "old interpretations" but only articulate and elaborate the dream that much the more.

I shall stress what Freud indicated but insufficiently emphasized. He was naturally interested in demonstrating how dreams could be interpreted, but knowing well that many in his audience believed that dreams were nonsensical, he minimized the radical act of free association, which not only divests the manifest content of the dream of its textural integrity but indicates its seminal power, since each dream image drives thousands of further associations that disseminate along a multitude of pathways. Think of my experience in the record store and how, in the course of free-associating, I recalled my son's school project. Further radiations of meaning derive from that intensity: my father's Greek father lived in Alexandria; the Bollas family left Chios in the mid-nineteenth century to avoid further Turkish massacres of its citizens. Out of these associations spring, in turn, further deconstructions: to my grandfather and his life, to what it means to be Greek, to Egypt as a place of dense conflict for me. And so on and so on. If we look back, now, to the moment when I entered the record store, we can see something of how this unit of experience was so psychically intense. I hesitated at the door. The sight of the Glass record in the store window initiated a highly complex inner experience that would have defied conscious consideration, although I maintain that all the ideas which I have teased out of that experience were there, in my unconscious, and were part of why this experience became an intensity. Had I walked past the same store on another day and seen a display of records of *Tosca*, I would not have endured such an evocative moment, pregnant with so many latent thoughts.

Unconscious mental life becomes more complex, and truer to its nature, it seems to me, if we also bear in mind that prior to passing the record store I am disseminating the free questions of the previous day, which were, in turn, sponsored by that evening's dreams. In the course of a day's experience, while walking along the street, I am unconsciously following differing strands of thought that are part of the act of free-associative dissemination. This dissemination articulates movements of desire, the self traveling thousands of ideational routes, leading not to nowhere, but to otherwhere, to an explosive creation of meanings, which nonetheless meet up with new units of life experience, and—as with the sight of the Glass recording—may become part of the formation of new psychic intensities.

———

The realization that we are all living disseminations of questioning complexities—arranged through our idioms' encounters with reality—and that our psychic meanderings create new and deeply textured psychic intensities suggests to me that when Freud invented his theory of the dream, he also fashioned a theory of all unconscious self experience.

What is that experience? If we take the dream as the median point, then the process begins with the subject's encounter in *le vécu*, when he "has" psychically intense experiences. These give birth to latent thoughts that demand representation. The dream work organizes them into images that further condense the day's experience, making room, for the most part, for aspects of the experienced. But upon remembering the dream, the free-associative process disseminates the work of condensation into its radiating pathways, and the trains of thought go roaring off in different directions, displacing the forged unities of dream condensation or the original pregnant intensities of the day, which are now deconstructed by all the elements that went into their interrogating vividness.

This entire process takes place on a smaller scale, if I may put it that way. The dream is not the only place of excited condensation in which psychic intensities are transformed by representations that give birth to trains of thought. Back to the record store. I see the Glass album and am excited by it: it gives rise to an urge that releases questions. I stand halfway in the doorway. I withdraw. I enter on impulse. Oral and phallic excitations are present: a libidinal moment is at hand. I think of my son's project. I have a vague sense of Egypt and my family, but it is displaced by many other thoughts.

To be more accurate, but also more complex, the order of associations I have presented in terms of the consideration of whether to buy the Glass album or not is misleading because, in order to make it clear, I have suggested a sequence, though the emerging thoughts were virtually simultaneous. There was a concurrence of thought on differing planes of psychic reality, an overlapping, occasioned by the evocative object: the album and "its" experience—and this concrescence of factors transcends any single element, transforming the episode into a meditation full of questions. Such moments feel psychically dense because, saturated with simultaneously evoked planes of unconscious ideation occurring at the same time, they provoke a kind of not unpleasant turbulence. We all know the sense of relief with which such an episode concludes, when one leaves the record store to continue on one's journey.

The conclusion of such an intensity is its boundary. Up to a point such intensities have the structure of the dream: condensations of latent ideas, mini-dreams. Afterward the person unknowingly is driven by dynamic questions as he free-associates. The vast majority of such inner associations are unconscious, although there are derivatives in consciousness, and such associations are in the form of conscious contemplations of differing elements evoked by the experience. So I might think of minimalist music, or of my friend whose brother-in-law plays in Glass's group. I might then simply leap over a chain of associations and think about Chios. Such leaps are, in fact, a part of the ordinarily explosive nature of free associations, rather as intensities create psychic bangs which create small but complex universes of thought.

Freud went on to indicate how such psychic moments demanded further representation by gaining access to dream imagery, but my more limited point is that the structure of the entire dream experience has its equivalent in ordinary waking life. We walk about, have intense moments, and then associate to them. We cohere as intensity, we disseminate as association. Walking about, cohering, disseminating. An oscillation that is simultaneous with other occurring coherences and disseminations, so that psychic life happens on intersecting planes of experience.

Imagine that before going to the record store I stopped to buy a paper. I see the headline "Clinton Wins Presidency," which is an intense moment for me, with many latent thoughts distilled into the emotion that lasts a few minutes. As I continue, I disseminate aspects of that intensity through unconscious, preconscious, and conscious elaborations. Imagine that just as I arrive at the record store I have been lost in thinking about Clinton and Kennedy, and an image of the Kennedy Center for the Performing Arts comes to mind. We can easily see, then, how this chain of association is part of the desire to buy the Glass recording, as a kind of antecedent though not a sole determinant. The sight of *Akhenaten* has, in itself, been sufficiently evocative to create a new psychic intensity, which after I depart from the record store leaves me the quiet acts of dissemination before the next moment of intense meaning.

My account of the experience is, of course, incomplete and I cannot hope to do justice to what is absent by embarking on a phenomenology of the self's immediate experiencings. But there is an important form of punctuation: all the ideas, visual images, auditory shapes, somatic registrations, evoked memories, libidinal propensities, floating weighted words, are punctuated by what Blanchot (1969) terms an "essential nothingness," which, changing its shape and function from moment to moment, silences the registers of sense. What is between the dialectics of being and nothingness? he asks. "A nothingness more essential than Nothingness itself—the void of an interval that continually hollows itself out and in hollowing itself out becomes distended: *the nothing as work and movement*" (italics mine) (7).

In the course of ordinary self experience I lose grasp of my thoughts, am interrupted by forgettings, frustrated by my failure to find a word for itself, stopped in the effort to think a thought that refuses as yet to come into cognition. In the background of my mind are glimmers of images and words, unheeded in consciousness as I concentrate on other matters—discarded mental contents that seem to slide into darkness. That nothingness is always there, whether it momentarily mutes speech, swallows up memory, refuses to yield an idea struggling to come into thought, or receives all the faint and discarded images and words that pass by in the back of my mind on an endless conveyor belt, from the unconscious passing briefly through consciousness to oblivion.

Nothing as work and movement is the place of defense in psychoanalysis; and there is an aesthetics of nothingness, in which the movement of the individual's nothingness accompanies lived experience and is transformed into negative hallucination, denial, repression, and riddance (splitting off).

The movement of nothing is essential to lived experience. Nothing is a presence that can be felt, as different in its forms as the dissemination of theories. In "The Snow Man," Wallace Stevens writes:

> For the listener, who listens in the snow,
> And nothing himself, beholds
> Nothing that is not there and the Nothing that is (10)

Each inner intensity bears the mark of the nothing which immediately precedes it and follows it. We are not in continuous unbroken discourse with our self, but, rather, *constantly* breaking the textures of inner experience with the movement of nothingness, with abrupt questions, diversions, turning points, ruptures, and elisions, and these are part of the pattern of the inevitably tattered fabric of being.

A theory of wakeful unconscious life, then, suggests a continuous simultaneous oscillation between psychic in-

tensities (cohesions) and their disseminations (fragmentations); Freud's terms "condensation" and "displacement"
designate these actions. If we think further about displacement we are led to a new understanding of the radical
breakage of coherence that is intrinsic to dissemination:
specifically, any idea (or condensation of ideas) cracks up
upon subsequent thought, as it gives way to a plenitude
of divergent and differing signifiers.

Back once more to the record store. I trust that I have
established that an ordinary encounter of the kind I have
discussed is a kind of psychic *bang* which pushes mental
contents into vastly different moving constellations. Some
of the chains of ideas are easily followed, but in fact, there
are often apparent gaps in the linkage. So from the sight
of *Akhenaten* I could find myself thinking of Chios. But
the next free association might be to getting a haircut. Is
the link obvious? I could, in retrospect, suggest one: that
Chios sponsored the notion of Greek and that on the
street I saw a Greek barbershop.

As Lacan teaches us, however, each signifier has a life
of its own. The phonemic structure of Chios may give rise
in me to leaping associations: to "key" and "host." I may
then wonder what food to buy for guests coming to dinner
at the end of the week. The word "Akhenaten" may
trigger other signifiers: "Ah," "nay," "eaten," "nation,"
"notion." The mind operates as a lexicon of association,
throwing up differing trains of thought, some of which
live only briefly in the unconscious, others of which reach
full consciousness and then lie about in the preconscious,
linking up to other associations, possibly to form "a
complex"—an organization of feelings, ideas, images, and
so forth that make some kind of sense to the unconscious.

The soma is involved in the act of utterance. "Glass" is

a smooth word launched by a guttural "G." The soft ending, however, may feel somatically unconvincing. "Akhenaten" is a more complex somatic action. "Ah" is a sound of surprise: it fits the sight of the record in the window. "Good," the soma might utter. But there is a "nay" present: an antithesis. Stuck between the "Ah" and the "nay" is a guttural "k" that rather sticks in one's throat. The "ten" sound, so far as the soma is concerned, may be a necessary conclusion to the signifier's somatic effect. "Ten" might play its part as an act of decision. The body ends its conflict with timpani!

Lacan's theory of the signifier indicates a logic oper-ating through the structure of language, and even if it is less easy to see the same act of dissemination in a sequence of visual images, abstract ideas, affects, or somatic se-quences, his understanding of the symbolic allows us to appreciate the thousands of separate logical evolutions that burst from a single event, each within its own logical chain but many of which leap over sentences, paragraphs, and pages to future links already known to be within the chain.

————

When I speak of displacement as an act of dissemination, I am trying to identify this unique process of *logical fragmentation* that bursts from psychically intense moments. Dissemination refers to a kind of dialectic: as person A encounters object B, A splits into separate ideational parts each with its own logical valorization. B has inspired A's split. But the outcome is not a synthesis between A and B or a compromise formation between the integrity of B and the integrity of A. Alternately, however, the splits that occurred in A could not have occurred without confrontation with B—or should one say except through

B? So A's encounter with B is rather like a moment of conception. Each idea is a kernel of some truth. As we speak the idea, it gives birth to other thoughts, each of which is itself a new kernel of yet another truth.

Take the word "tree." It signifies a growing plant of a type that will readily come to the mind of most people uttering the word. But there are other ideas within this signifier which take us elsewhere. The tree of life, for example, might take me into either a contemplation on the meaning of existence or to a consideration of my genealogy. I am writing this paragraph a few days after Christmas, and if someone asked me how our tree was a few days ago, it would have brought to mind a Christmas tree. Phonemically, "tree" may evoke "three," a number with a disseminative destiny of unusual power in our civilization. And there is also the idiomatic significance of any signifier to the individual: "my" signifiers will be different from someone else's. As we meet up with objects—literally a tree, or the word "tree"—the signifier divides into separate ideas, which in turn divide into still other ideas: in the beginning may be the word, but in the end is a Babel of divergent intellections.

Freud's theory of displacement would have us believe that any act of dissemination inevitably carried within it the content of the original idea, now displaced. According to his topographical model, the ideal solution would be for the displaced idea to be close to its original latent source, although if it were a noxious idea, it might need to be put quite far down the chain of associations before it was allowed to come into full consciousness. So, for example, an individual who has had a moment's unconscious discomfort when considering a sexual act he would fully disown were it to reach consciousness intercedes on the level of preconscious action and comes up with a more remote and permissible idea: the wish to see a certain film that features an erotically arousing actress. One cannot dispute Freud's concept of displacement as it describes the nature of a precise psychic action, but what he does not directly address, it seems to me, is the movement any logic of displacement sets into action: once a pathway for an idea is set up, even if a substitute idea is found for the noxious idea, this train of thought will have subdivided along the way, giving rise to other notions and interests —so the deconstruction of a wish is part of the process of thinking itself. *The unconscious breaks up its own desire.* It fulfills wishes by thinking, but the process of thought becomes suffused with the logic of unconscious action: in this instance, the contents of desire are deconstructed by the erotics of form. The wish to have a sexual relation with a certain woman, a wish too toxic to enter consciousness, is a mental content that is partly fulfilled by the wish to see an actress in a film. The mental content of the wish is partly gratified, but at the same time, the ego's decision to set the wish on a given formal journey—selecting a genre of film, rather than, say, reading or walking in the park—is a kind of erotics of form that dissolves the wish at the very moment of gratifying it.

Mental freedom—the urge to free-associate and to disseminate one's wishes and needs through a chain of ideas with no terminal point but with aesthetic intelligence—is a form of desire that supports but supplants the specific desires driven by instinctual life.

Acts of dissemination—chains of ideas, phonemic slides, somatic choices, and pathemes (in which the individual changes course on the basis of the logic of affect)—lead to continuous subdivisions, an infinity of devolutions from the originating psychic intensity, and this invisible tree of branches and leaves is in itself an erotics of form. Were we able to see it, and we never shall, we would witness an aesthetic movement which articulates and elaborates the idiom of the self that we are and its destiny.

Free associations to the psychic intensities of everyday life set the individual on a kind of psychic splitting, valorizing differing interests on separate pathways of dissemination that continually divide and then subdivide again, so that no one meeting up with the next state of affairs that occasions a psychic intensity does so as a blank screen. I set out from the record store on my way to the library, lost in thoughts—or the disseminative thinkings that occur as a result of my psychic intensity—and by the time I reach the library I am, as it were, a rather dispersed being. Which of my variegated disseminations will link with the new intensity that occurs in the library? Perhaps in the forty-five minutes of this journey, one train of thought has taken me to Alexandria (synonymous with a great library), another to Lawrence Durrell, who wrote *The Alexandria Quartet*, another to my brother, whose middle name is Alexander, another to the construction of the British Museum and to an architect—James Stirling—who died recently. I begin my psychic journey with an originating intensity and then am flung into various far corners of thought and feeling, deeply lost from my consciousness yet cognitively alert and aware of my surroundings.

At some point (and where is it?) the realization that I am now almost at the library occurs to me. I am already aware that I will look up the literature on confidentiality, and I have had many thoughts on the book I am writing, with a friend, on the erosion of confidentiality in the practice of psychoanalysis and psychotherapy in the

United States. These trains of thought were set in motion the day before when I was inspired (a psychic intensity) by the urge to go to the library, but now, in the ensuing episodes of life, events have intervened, and as I approach the library I do so rather lost in those thoughts that were inspired by being in the record store and reading the notes on the opera. Yet somewhere, in what Winnicott termed the intermediate area of experience, here between two locations, my disseminations are meeting up with prior disseminations (from the night before) and curious sorts of psychic marriages are occurring. I did not intend to think of Durrell at the library. Nor did I intend to pop down to the Egyptian room to have a quick look. But I do. And these actions are derivative of the episode forty-five minutes before. They bear no direct relation to my literature search on confidentiality, but nonetheless they are part of my experience of the library that day.

All that I have described is *in* consciousness, and yet the truth is that most of what takes place in such moments occurs unconsciously. If one is free to be disseminated—and in Chapter 4 I shall discuss the problems attending on this—then the individual will encounter new objects, or old objects subject to new intentions, with a complex set of dense inner chains of interest, some of which will, by accident, coincide with other, prior pathways: this psychic texture is the basis of anyone's depth of mind. It is entirely a matter of whether one can or cannot experience a psychically intense moment and then, crucially, whether one can be lost in thought when the nucleus of the experience explodes along fissures of separating and dividing interest. If this occurs, then one will approach new experiences in life *in-formed*, rendered into a being with depth, precisely because one has been flung in the same spell of time to the far corners of one's universe, traversing many memories, bearing instinctual traces, exploring new object connections, and thinking by associating that which cannot be gathered into consciousness.

But what happens when the individual is lost in thought? Are those moments of free-associative dissemination, when the person rides out the journeys of the mind, occasions of mental intensity? Oddly enough, no. For in riding the Underground, gazing at a passenger here and a person there, I think of Glass, of Egypt, of Chios, and then look at a newspaper headline, which, like all the other cognitive observations, is intermissionary to my other mental perambulations. Can I characterize the nature of my inner experience during such moments of being lost in thought? I know I cannot. They are not clear. For every image there are several partial and unrealized movements toward image. For every visualization there are a multitude of unvisualized yet assumed images that contribute to the feel of dense imagining. For every contemplated word there are scores of other words which never reach consciousness but which have been part of the movement of language. And so the account continues, with each and every element that goes into the making of self experience.

Indeed, I would like to strengthen the image of being lost in thought. I think these are the moments when we are in the heart of darkness, dispersed into so many elements that constitute being that from the point of view of consciousness we are no longer present. These absences, or abstentions from alert existence, are, in my view, vital to the elaboration of one's idiom, which is deeply dependent upon the articulations and elaborations that occur during wakeful dreaming. We do not need to chant a single word or join a religious sect with a dreamy-eyed guru to know what Eastern religions mean by the need for the ego to dissolve: I think I know what is meant, and each of us, if we are fortunate to be in a state of health, is able to do just that. We can enter a form of solitude in which we are lost in thought, and then lost to thought, and then lost to the elements of our being that move in disseminating articulations of discrete interests.

A psychic intensity, then, is a momentous condensation in which many truths are conjured, often through the evocative effect of an object. To use another Freudian term, it is an overdetermined episode, frequently the point of convergence of prior displacements. It bears desire in its very structure and is pregnant with possibilities. After its experiencing, when the individual is outside the spell of the epiphanic, the desires which converged break free with energy borrowed from the act of convergence. Belief in the moment of truth, provided by any psychic intensity, is displaced by the breakup of any such truth into divergent interests which are suggestive of still other truths to come.

Freud's theory of displacement described a transference of energy. An idea unacceptable to consciousness and therefore doubly charged—with its own valorization and the antiforces of consciousness—displaced its energy to another, more remote and possibly more acceptable idea. The new idea, now accepting the transferred energy, would therefore have more of a charge to it than an idea that had not been subjected to this transfer. Although this concept has been of less clinical interest to psychoanalysts in recent decades, one can see Freud trying to conceptualize the nature of mental intensity. After all, if an individual has a psychically intense experience during the day, the feelings and ideas which have composed that moment will have been subjected to a different type of mental investment than more simply cognitive moments, when the subject is simply perceiving reality and not *undergoing* a psychically intense moment. Thus in thinking of the energy that is released by such moments we see how a concept of energy or mental investment is of use, given that the subsequent free associations will have been driven by the passion aroused in the discrete psychic intensity.

Dissemination reflects the desire to elaborate the idiom of one's being. In Beethoven's work, say, we can hear the development of *his* musical idiom and can also hear the far-flung idea, the invention. A development which is also an invention suggests a logic that is not solely predetermined, but subject to moments of inspiration that offer an element of one's personal being in a new variation that further deploys the self at the very moment of changing it. But the musical analogy is too simplistic. Beethoven's complete works can be organized according to various themes and interests and we will find a unity there. Human mental life does not have such a compositional unity to it, although narrative unities can be constructed about people's lives. Instead, I think we endure millions of psychic intensities in our life: we have tens of thousands of dreams, we are flung along millions of chains of association, which are never lost upon the unconscious, although what emerges as the result of this journey is not a unitary phenomenon but rather a vast network of desires, memories, interests, curiosities, conflicts, and accidents that simply have been lived by us.

What do we disperse, then, when we disseminate idiom? Trains of thought each leading to an infinite declension, which in the end circles back on the individual: disbanded, loosed upon the world as our investment, are we not theories which meet up with experiences that raise us into questions? Equipped from birth with a theorizing intelligence unique to yourself, your personal form becomes an interrogative action when it encounters the other. "What is that?" "Who is that?" "What am I?" "Who am I?" As Blanchot wrote (1969), when Oedipus confronted the Sphinx he embodied man's relation to himself as an enigma: as we move through our life we do so as a personality, a unique set of evolving theories generating insights and new perspectives, but meeting up with experience that turns our self as theory into increasing sets of questions.

The psychoanalyst and his patient therefore set loose far more questions than either can answer, but these in turn increase the ability of the analysand's unconscious to deploy its idiom. If unconscious thinking is too complex to be grasped by consciousness, if one person's unconscious can communicate with another's unconscious mind only by playing with it, then psychoanalysis is a radical act— freeing the subject from character restraints and intersubjective compliances through the naturally liberating and expressive medium of free association. However essential the psychoanalyst's interpretations may be, however useful a patient's self-discoveries are, the fundamental agency of change in a psychoanalysis is the continuous exercise of this freedom, which ultimately deconstructs and disseminates any narrative action (whether rendered by the psychoanalyst or by his patient) and establishes in place of the morality of the thematic a dissembling spirit that plays the self into myriad realities. All along, what has seemed to be the means to truth—free association—is the

truth itself, which psychoanalysis can bring to its patients.*
In this moving expression of unbound ideas, the patient
not only finds self-expression but, more tellingly, finds or
rediscovers the route to unconscious freedom and personal
creativity.

---

* Barratt has written that it is not interpretation that is the royal road to the
unconscious, but "the 'royal road' is free associative discourse itself, not whatever
this discourse may seem to be 'about' " (198).

4

Preoccupation
unto Death

Psychoanalysts come across many people who lack the unconscious freedom necessary for creative living. Their freedom is restricted, their mind bound in anguished repetitions that terminate the dissemination of the self.

This obstruction to freedom is easily observed in the person who is obsessed. This may be an obsession with body weight, as in anorexia or bulimia, or an obsession with personal hygiene, or it may be an intense preoccupation with a husband or a wife who is incessantly railed against. Often a lament about the workplace will dominate the analytical session day after day. What we are considering here is *any* obsession that keeps from the analytical consulting room the kind of dissemination one can observe in other patients. Of course, although a patient may suffer from a kind of obsessional neurosis, and talk about his isolations of affect and his compulsive rituals, he may still be free to experience psychically intense occasions, to condense himself into deep unconscious meanings, and to have bursts of inspired trains of thought enabling him to live a more creative life. The problem I am addressing here borrows the signifier that we associate with a particular disorder, but I shall use it in a somewhat different way, to illustrate how such obsessions preclude the ability to participate in the unconscious rhythms of everyday experience.

There are patients who rigorously sustain an intense and unrelenting obsession with something which is unmovable by interpretation. Such people remain wedded to their obsessions for an unusually long time, sometimes to the very end of the analysis, even in modified form. The analyst's enterprise is a frustrating one, accentuated not only by the patients' craving for the obsessional object, but by the total indifference shown to analytical insight directed toward *any* understanding.

For example, I once analyzed a woman who rarely let a session go by without complaining about her husband, and even though the analysis was productive and worthwhile, her complaints about her husband continued unabated for many years. Along the way she learned a lot in the analysis: she dreamed complex and interesting dreams, she recovered lost screen memories (which had been "whited out" because of her incessant thoughts about the husband), and she gained sufficient psychic space to think about other people in life, including her children, colleagues at work, and a law practice for which she received increasing public recognition.

We understood how the descriptions of her husband objectified unwanted aspects of herself. This was not difficult. She repeatedly stated that she was a weak person, lacking conviction, frightened of others, and socially uncouth: the very things she went on and on about in criticizing her husband. As the years ticked by, I got so good at interpreting her that I could almost literally catch a projective identification in midcourse. One day after lamenting her anxieties about her own inadequacies she said, "But of course . . ." and I interrupted to say "and now it is going into your husband, isn't it," and of course it was. These amusing interjections were not unimportant to the therapeutic alliance. And she did learn about her projective processes and how her husband contained the unwanted parts of herself: she saw how it gave her a sense of partial mastery in that she dominated him and thus had a kind of pseudo-control over the unwanted portions of herself; she also recognized that by mistreating her unwanted parts, she could be abusive in a safe environment, because her husband was symbiotically devoted to her.

But the obsession continued. She would tell me, however briefly, of the previous day's or evening's personality malpractice by her husband, describing him with an unforgiving eye: how he had tried clumsily and awkwardly to help one of her children dress and had put the child's clothing on inside out, persisting against evidence of failure. Reports of this kind painted a picture of a somewhat out-of-touch person who, however well-intentioned, appeared to live a highly distracted life, exactly like my patient. Other times I would be told of what he failed to do. Coming home from a very difficult day at the office, she told him of her woes, to which he replied, "Oh well, dear, it can be like that, can't it," leaving her enraged by his phatic empathy. Sometimes she would almost ceremoniously interrupt herself to say that she could see that what she had just said about him echoed what she herself had done that day, and on rare occasions she could link her anxieties over his insensitivity to her projection of them onto her husband. But these exercises were really introjections of the analytical perspective in spite of herself, as in truth she always needed to situate herself in relation to her husband's person.

After many years of working with her, the phrase "preoccupation unto death" crossed my mind. What on earth was I thinking of? I knew, of course, what I meant by preoccupation. That was obvious. But why death? I recollected a period of time in the analysis in which the differing theories of the death instinct had been in the forefront of my analytical mind as I tried to analyze—perhaps quite effectively—the patient's deadening of herself and her psyche through the construction of a deadened object, a kind of circuit of doom. Work in that area had been meaningful, and had enabled us to make important links to the patient's early development. So why return, now, to the phrase "preoccupation unto death"?

Some time passed and I could then see that my interest in the natural work of unconscious life directed my attention toward those clinical problems that stalled such processes. What did it mean, in terms of that rhythm of unconscious creativity, that some persons were able to stop it, to prevent it from moving in its natural cycle? That was the problem that I took back to my sessions with my patient—a part, shall we say, of my countertransference.

I could see that my analysand could not bear to let herself surrender to the processes intrinsic to unconscious creativity. She prevented all but the very rare psychically intense moment to occur, instead substituting *false psychic intensities* which inevitably took the form of an affective response to her husband. I realized, in fact, that she frequently complained about this. She had told me many times that she wished she could experience something intensely—anything. Her desire to be less disconnected from feelings and emotions had led her to try all manner of expressive therapies, yelling a bit here and there, dancing elsewhere, dramatizing possibilities in cuddly Gestalt consulting rooms, but all to no avail.

But she was no stoic. Hating her husband conjured up powerful emotions that gave her a reason for existence. Positive emotions were mistrusted, because love left her feeling as if she were coming apart, losing any sense of inner coherence: hate organized her, gave her purpose. Meaningful work had been done in understanding this aspect of her life; still, the obsession continued.

It became apparent that in relation to her husband, one of the two had to be useless in order that the other person could have some sort of life, the assumption being that if two persons were both fully alive, they would soon lose control and come to a catastrophic end. The husband, then, was not so much a transitional object, used to assist the self in moving forward toward deployment of the self's idiom into the object world, but more a terminal object, selected because it ends the self's disseminative movement. Looking back, I could see that the patient was made anxious by creative work between the two of us and stopped it by seeming to have no recollection of the previous session. By focusing obsessively on the behaviors of her husband, she picked a terminal object that ended the natural forward movement of those departing trains of thought that are the elaborations of any person's idiomatic experience of life. Clearly there was a dread of surrender to the rhythm of unconscious experiencing itself, a process which usually feels, or should feel, natural.

Why?

The adult whose childhood relationship with the mother

was secure can allow himself to deploy the "itness" inherent to his being in the supportive presence (and through the existence) of the other. Freud designated this "itness" id, and Winnicott used the term "true self," though I find the term "idiom" more apt. The adult who can experience his idiom will be able to surrender himself to the unconscious creation of experience, which in turn enriches that part of the self which is outside consciousness.

My patient suffered a severe and sharp trauma in the early years of her life, which in turn affected her mother's capacity to look after her. Her mother overcompensated for the debilitating depression she suffered by idolizing her child's body and being. Her fear of disappearing into the mother's excessive adoration of her was a very conscious anxiety, long preceding the analysis, and she worried that if she did not keep her mother at arm's length she would be consumed by her love. Instead she transformed her mother into a terminal object, only approaching her for essential needs, but avoiding her as an other to whom she could bring her thoughts and feelings. Where another child would collaborate with the mother in order to disseminate important inner experiences, she saw talking to the mother as an impossibility. Thus she did not have that important use of the mother as a sympathetic and inspiring other. She was unable to lose herself in the experience of an object, unable to develop her unconscious creativity. She felt shallow and out of touch with life's riches.

Obsession, from the Latin *obsessio*, for a very long time referred to the act of being possessed by an evil spirit. Later it defined an extreme of preoccupation, such as domination by an idea, desire, or emotion. To be obsessed, says Webster's, is to be haunted by an idea that troubles the mind.

Preoccupation, from the Latin *praeoccupare*, is a less intense form of mental repetition than obsession. Like the obsessed person, the preoccupied individual is very occupied with a particular idea, but there is an intriguing and informative difference. One of the ancient meanings of the word is to "occupy or take possession of (something) before someone else or beforehand." This suggests that the person must rush into a space before it is dominated by the other: there is anxiety in the act of pre-occupying.

My patient feared her mother would occupy her own mental spaces, and so protected herself by transforming the mother into an obsession of thought, which in turn created a hidden, alternative, and quite secret space: the place where a good mother would operate, leaving the analysand plenty of room in which to grow and develop because privacy was respected and ensured. As an alternative to introjecting the mother, which would mean allowing the mother into the child's inner space, the child pre-occupies this space with an obsessive objectification of the mother, rushing into the area for introjection with a projectively rigid characterization of the mother.

My patient also had a secret preoccupation, which thus far I have not mentioned. Fifteen years before beginning the analysis she had met a man at a professional conference and they had had a brief affair. Since that event, they would meet at an annual conference, during which time she would feel deeply in love with him. Her lover had not wanted to continue the affair, but he was exceedingly flirtatious and sustained a high degree of sexual excitation, so she was always at a strange kind of muted fever pitch when with him. During the year they would write and telephone one another, and she remained profoundly preoccupied with him. She wondered what he was up to, followed his every move in the professional world, was exceedingly jealous of his other female friends (he was steadfastly promiscuous), and had no sense of critical judgment in relation to his frequent professional misconduct.

We can see the difference here between my use of the terms "obsession" and "preoccupation." Her obsession with her husband's inadequacies led her to a tiresome, relentless, and deadening itemization of his conduct. One thought never proceeded naturally from the next, in the sense that no one listing of her husband's failure led *unconsciously* to another misdemeanor, such that one could observe some form of unconscious dissemination or elaboration. The items were terminal reports. But her preoccupation with her lover did allow for some "mental wanderings": she would wonder what he was doing, with whom he was spending time, and she would dwell on aspects of her cultural interests and occasionally elaborate on them.

Pathological obsession is aimed at maintaining a terminal object that *ends* all unconscious use of the object: ideational, affective, somatic, or transferential. A preoccupation allows for the migration of feelings into the situation: the object is subjected to use in that it is subjected to fantasy and can therefore elaborate aspects of the subject. My patient's preoccupation with her lover was to a fundamentally *absent* object, while the obsession with the husband was to a fundamentally *present* other. She had always been obsessed with a present other: first her mother, and subsequently her husband, both of whom were consistent parts of her daily life.

A preoccupied person has more internal mental space free to dwell on mental contents than an obsessed person. In this respect, the preoccupied patient does, in a certain way, create an internal space, into which she can rush with her own mental life, before anyone gets there. She preoccupies the internal space signified by the lover, with her own libidinal and ego wishes and needs. When she thinks of her husband, on the other hand, she feels haunted by a deeply disappointing and extremely irritated presence. The obsessed person feels impinged upon by the object; as in its ancient usage, it is like being taken over by a demon, driven crazy by an intrusive idea. The preoccupied person seems to do something rather different: he conjures a mental space into which he brings all of his interests—in this case one object—to the exclusion of all else.

It was not difficult to discuss with my patient the fact that she had divided her love and hate between two people, and that her obsession with her husband was an inverse of her preoccupation with her lover. She understood this. Over time the relation to her lover waned, as her affection for her husband increased, but it would be wrong to say that the obsession disappeared. In lessened form it remained. Whenever she was in a certain mood she would invoke the actions of her husband in order to terminate her own unconscious freedom.

It is fortunate for our study of the difference between preoccupation and obsession that both states existed in this patient, because it enables us to see more clearly, I think, that her preoccupation is nonetheless a schizoid reluctance to surrender to unconscious experiencing. Her lover's refusal of her desire more than protected her from that kind of elaborative deployment of the self's idiom that is achieved in the full course of a relationship. Her desires were always frustrated and her yearnings became repetitious inner states that merely mirrored the frustrations she had with her husband.

Obsession, preoccupation, and, as we shall see, passion are the objects of investigation in this chapter, but it would be folly to leave out the important center of a spectrum which I explore from one end of illness (obsession) to the other (passion). There is surely an ordinary kind of withdrawal from object relating, or uses of objects, to a particular focus on one object, or group of objects, for a limited and generative period of time.

From *concentrare*, close to the word *"concenter"* and related to the Latin *concentrum*, which breaks down into *con* (together) and *centrum* (center), to concentrate is to "bring to or collect toward a common center" or "to collect or gather as at a center." Mothers and fathers see this easily enough when children are engaged in a form of *concentration*, looking intently at an object, or busily at work constructing an object, or playing with others. Much of Winnicott's observational interest is in the child's concentration: the need to turn away from an object through hesitation to prepare for concentration on it, the value of unimpingement, and the essentials of solitude so that absolute focus on an object is possible in the first place.

My own interest in psychic genera could be considered in part a theory of unconscious concentration, for the gathering together in one psychic place of related but disparate and dispersed phenomena is a conceptualization of what happens when a center for psychic collection is created. We shall have to keep at the back of our minds, then, throughout this chapter, that there is a generative channeling of interest—a concentration—which assists unconscious exploration of the object world. It is not the subject of study here, but necessitates mention.

When she began her analysis, my patient was modestly successful in her career. It had, to some extent, been the object of a kind of preoccupation because for years and years she had felt herself a failure of sorts. In the beginning, her own complaints about her work would alternate with complaints about her partner, but as time went on, these diminished.

Indeed something rather secretive happened. She began to enjoy her work, spurred on in part by increased public recognition, but also by a sense of true accomplishment. In time she developed a passionate interest in her work, reading up on it, attending conferences, giving public lectures. Sessions were more lively. She talked less about her husband, because she was now so absorbed in her work. And it was also the case that each week she brought news about the self that had been triggered by her creative work life. She was surprised not only to discover capacities she thought she lacked but to take note of ill-perceived, destructive inclinations, particularly in the area of envy. She also recovered childhood memories that were evoked by work-related phenomena: I noticed that when she discussed her creative life, more memories, reflections, urges, and needs were released into consciousness than when she talked about her husband or lover.

In short, she had developed a *passionate* relation to an object. This word signifies a more complex mental state and designates a more intricate form of object relation than obsession or preoccupation. Its Indo-European base is *pe*, meaning to harm, and its Greek origin is *pema*, signifying destruction. These very early meanings of the word are, in my view, precursors to Winnicott's understanding of the child's passion as destructive, which he saw as crucial to the true self's use of an object. Passion also suggests pathos and suffering, certainly in its classical and medieval life as a signifier. Jesus is a figure who embodies passion as martyred sacrifice. The Latin word *paene*, which inherited one of the Greek derivatives, is closest to pathos. But then the concept became associated with *any* emotion, or expression of emotion. This is easy enough to see, I suppose, in that Jesus' suffering certainly is heightened by his emotive outburst toward his father for abandoning him to an earthly death. Eventually the word took on a modern usage. Passion came to mean an emotion that was compelling, even extreme, but it also identified a particular kind of excitement. Webster's four-step delineation of the word's contemporary meanings virtually traces its history: (a) great anger; rage; fury, (b) enthusiasm or fondness [a passion for music], (c) strong love or affection, (d) sexual drive or desire: lust.

It will be seen, however, that the course of a passion involves the individual in an intense preoccupation with an object, in which the integrity of the object—its character or value, as it were—has a most profound effect upon the subject. The object changes the subject. But it is an interesting type of transformation. I suggest that passionate object relations initially change the individual not through the mutative effect of introjection and insight, but rather through existential alteration to the subject's being, brought about by immersive engagement with the object at a deeply unconscious level of mutual effect. My patient, for example, did not gain what I think of as introjective insights in her analysis for a very long time and even then only minimally. She did not "take in" interpretations that would become preconscious insights, linking up with her own associations or subsequent thoughts; but she was nonetheless profoundly affected by the analytic process. *It* changed her; my interpretations did not. Of course, this is something of an absurdity, as my interpretations were a vital part of the process. But it was the full effect of the object relation that transformed her capacity for object usage—of the passionate kind—rather than analytical insight. Only when she could use analysis as an object could she then become interested in generative introjection of analytical interpretation.

So in describing a passion I am discussing a type of object usage that changes the individual but does not necessarily result in a more insightful subject. As we know, a person may be a passionate painter, composer, or car designer—his engagement with the object of his passion may affect him profoundly, enabling him to elaborate his or her own idiom—but he may be totally lacking in insight. We are talking, then, about a most particular change, which cannot necessarily even be analyzed, although it will take place in some form within the analysis, and is also available for psychoanalytical deconstruction, even if such intellections would be lost to the patient upon delivery.

———

Roger was Swiss. His father was a Spanish composer and his mother was a university professor in Switzerland. He was on the verge of hospitalization when he came to analysis. This tall, blond, sixteen-year-old was not eating, and his weight was dangerously low. As with so many anorexics, he displayed the customary indifference to his condition, which for some odd reason, he noted, was a curious preoccupation of others. Yes, he admitted, he was obsessed with food, but he felt that the obsession was more silly than its object—it was foolish to worry so much—and that his parents and others (including me) were more stupid than he was, for now we were all getting into *it*.

Nonetheless, he was not keen to go to the hospital, so he reluctantly agreed to be weighed each day, and a minimum weight was set. If he went below that weight, he would go to the hospital, but the assessment of weight and the decision to send him to the hospital would be entirely taken by his physician, so it was really not part of the analysis. I cannot detail this adolescent's deconstruction of food, except to say that it rivaled in some ways Lévi-Strauss's *The Raw and the Cooked*, as he subjected each piece of food to a kind of linguistic deconstruction, placing it in its order of signifiers. A "peach," for example, *did* raise a question about whether Prufrock was somehow right. It was an object that confronted one with a certain daring. It signified youth, vulnerability, fuzz but no hair, and it brought to mind "peachy" as a description of a certain person. But with an almost equivalent force, Roger could suddenly suspend all such deconstructive interest: a peach would simply be "a piece of food with skin on it" and he would describe trying to eat it, picking away at the skin, observing its interior, discovering the pit, and finding it strangely unfoodlike—more an abstraction of what food was meant to be. As he had no hunger in the first place, it seemed absurd to eat something that was only an abstraction of the concept of eating. What was the point?

Each piece of food was capable of either a linguistic-cultural deconstruction or a reduction to total insignificance.

He was an exceptionally intelligent, intellectually gifted young man, whose adolescent narcissism was quite heady, to say the least; and although I found him vulnerable and likable, he had only a few friends, and a good many people thought him insufferable. He did not make himself any more personable by incessantly describing the world and its events—including the people in it—as very "boring." Nothing interested him, although he was always somewhat excited by his own scathing denunciations of differing situations. His weight loss had produced an androgyne look. I said I thought he preferred to remain a boy, and how becoming a young man was unacceptable, as he wished always to bask in the idolizing light of the mother's love. His acute anorexia began after he was rebuffed by a girl on a scuba-diving holiday; but in fact, the trauma had been not the girl, but the arrival of sexual fantasies and their intensities, which he was able to decathect through the anorexic accomplishment of denuding the body of any desire, and then turning it into a kind of abstraction of the body. He found my emphasis on his anorexic strategy only barely sufferable, but he never denied the interpretations I offered, and I could see that he even found them somewhat intriguing, while claiming it was all still *very, very boring.*

One session when he was telling me how absurd the world was, I said to him that he must be referring to Camus's theory of the absurd. He replied, "*Who* is Camus?" I said, "You mean, you—who find this world so boring and who have been fatigued to the point of narcolepsy at school—don't know who Camus was?" I said this in a slightly joshing and amused way. "No, I don't. Well anyway, what did he write? I could read it, and I will tell you what I think." That week he "consumed" Camus's writing, reading in ten days everything written by Camus that had been translated into English. This led to Sartre, who in turn led to Heidegger, who led of course to Kant, and by the end of the term, Roger was reading Greek philosophy, devouring the works of centuries like an avaricious cynic eating up the world's great philosophical texts.

We did not abandon the analysis, and I continued to

wait for news from his unconscious life, which was meager but occasionally forthcoming. But something different was taking place. Characteristically he would come to a session, flop in the chair, and tell me he had just read, let's say, Augustine, whom he found "maybe interesting" but not much. I would ask him to tell me what he thought of the reading and he would usually give me a brilliant account; I would then often challenge his view, or question some conclusion.

Now here was a situation in which *mind*, as Winnicott said, was separated out from *psyche* and from *soma*. I *engaged* his mind and transformed intellection into a certain kind of scene for the spontaneous expression of thoughts, associations, confusions, and feelings. Meanwhile he developed a passionate interest in philosophy, in fact he educated himself rather remarkably, and in turn recathected other intellectual disciplines (he graduated in art history), enabling him to pass his exams, when previously all of us were certain he would fail.

Philosophical texts (and later literary, anthropological, and historical works) had become passionate objects for him, but by entering the passionate place, as it were, I resituated the object *from* the purely schizoid intrapsychic usage *to* the shared schizoid usage (initially) until eventually the passionate object desisted as a thing in itself, and the object relation—discussing, arguing, idealizing, hating, etc.—emerged in its place. Roger then became capable of ordinary concentration and withdrew into object usage for generative purposes.

Roger's evolution in the analysis proceeded from an obsession (the anorexia) to a transient preoccupation, to a passion, and eventually to concentration. By transforming the nature of the object usage, but not the energy behind the use, he nonetheless moved from the anti-relating of manipulation of the terminal object, to usage of an object as a thing in itself, and to realization of the structure or integrity of objects which changed him. Certainly one can see here inklings of what Winnicott means by use of the transitional object, but to me it is stretching things too far to use his important concept to describe what the object was that was so useful to Roger: it requires a different naming. I wish to assign the name *integral object* to describe the value of an object as a thing in itself, where its integrity allows the individual to be nourished by its usage. This term seeks to define an unconscious perception of the object as a thing in itself. The object is not only a container which receives the subject's projective identifications but a thing with a structure which when used has a specific (even if individual) effect upon the person. When a person finds that engagement with the structure of an object is the aim of his desire, and appreciates something of its specifically nourishing value, then I believe the individual has discovered the use of the object's integrity.

The object of pathological obsession is a purely projective container into which the individual evacuates his psychic life in order to terminate contact with it. The object of a preoccupation is somewhere in between a purely projective and a structural use and may qualify as a form of transitional object. The *concentration* is there, as Winnicott found with infants, as is the *intense interest* in the object, and one can see the emergence of love and hate, even a type of passion. But the individual conjures an object of such interest in order to pre-occupy the potential space of a more liberated object usage, betraying those anxieties that generate such a move on the part of the ego. Use of the object as a structure, employed for its specific character, reflects an unconsciously perceived differentiation between what that object can offer as opposed to any other object. I am reluctant to assign it a developmental virtue, as I think individuals along a wide spectrum of diagnoses have the capacity for object usage at this level. But it serves our purpose here to see how obsessive, preoccupied, and passionate object relations differ although they share the same spectrum. In that respect, the individual's unconscious discovery of the integral object may allow for passionate usage of the object, and transform the negative energy of obsession to the positive energy of passion.

Winnicottians might argue that the integral thing is, in fact, a transitional object. Certainly the passionate engagement with an object's structure rings true to the definition of the transitional object. Indeed it is possible that all along one of the reasons why the transitional object is so passionately embraced is that it stands for that interchange between subject and object that testifies to the creative transformations of self achieved through the use of the object.

But there is a slight but important step just beyond the transitional. It is akin to a separate sense, in which the individual unconscious recognizes that any one object has a specific structure that makes its use for the subject transformationally distinct. This use of the object describes *processes evoked* by the subject's *engagement* with different types of experience in reality: reading a book will have a different effect upon oneself than listening to music; gazing at a painting will evoke a different set of internal responses than playing volleyball. These "objects" have differing structures, and in this respect are almost exactly the opposite of the transitional object, which is one thing standing, as it were, in the place of all things to come and all things that have been. The passionate object, however, does bear kinship with the transitional object: there is a single-minded devotion to this one thing which in the adult may be music, writing, designing cars, or whatever. Writers will describe their vocation as a form of illness, as do artists, car freaks, and surfers. This may be true, to a point, particularly when the passionate object seems to occupy too much of the individual's unconscious investment.

The infant who finds the transitional object falls passionately in love with a thing. But such falling is generative because he establishes the right to passionate existence through an intimate relation to the object of use. Winnicott assumes that such ruthless use of objects derives from a generative intimacy even if such employment is primitive —e.g., "I love you so much I could eat you up." Love and hate are fused through the discovery and use of the transitional object, and its significance fades when the child has fully grasped his or her right to use objects as matters of desire.

But does the object of passion terminate that unconscious freedom of which I have written? Yes and no. Use of the object enables the subject to change significantly: to become more joyful, discover new perspectives, and so on. Nonetheless, it may restrict the individual from developing a more multifaceted personality. We should also remember that passionate use of an object is the end point of a spectrum that begins with obsession, even though such illness may unleash creativity!

An object relation which is passionate rather than obsessional may be equally disturbed. We can see this in the individual who is passionate about opera but seems addicted to the aesthetic differences between its objects.

Something is wrong here. The individual has lost his

own subjectivity by falling into the structure of the object. The obsessive acts similarly, but while he falls into the object as container of his own projections, the passionate person falls into the erotics of difference, which, ironically, obliterates his subjectivity. At this point we may ask whether these passions are not closer to perversions. Here the object is vehemently pursued and apparently capitulated to in order to gain control over the nature of difference—a difference not only between self and other but between objects. By fetishizing an object (e.g., opera, car, boat, computer) until it becomes a passion, the individual may be attacking its differentness. He embraces in order to forget.

Daniel Stern's (1985) research on infants reveals that babies have an intrinsic interest in what is "new," a precursive appreciation of the integrity of objects. A child who meets up with a new object that announces its difference from other known objects may concentrate on it. In doing so, the child unconsciously invests considerable interest in it, gets lost in it, and uses—or works—it as an occasion for personal transformation: something we call knowledge.

This concentrated interest in new objects is essential for individual development. But ironically, although the object is what matters, through its use by the subject it becomes transformed into an elaboration of the individual's subjectivity. Once used it is forgotten, although its particular psychic status will be stored in the unconscious as a thing *transformed and transforming*. I may discover a new book and read it, but in my doing so, both the book and I are transformed.

For the person who has begun to use objects to elaborate and articulate the self, *life is now considered as an object*. It is the next step after discovery of the transitional object. Unless the transitional object is invested with a passion leading to its fetishization, it is used to establish the *principle of universal use*. The adult who has reached that stage will consciously think of his or her life as a distinct object and will consider how to use it, and though this will not determine *how* that life is used, it does herald the arrival of an unconscious attitude.

People whose experiences enable them to reach this point realize that using objects engages the self with other structures that affect their own idiom and are also necessary for the idiom to disseminate itself. We can see how some people's lives are informed by this. They seek out new objects and experiences, or they re-experience the familiar in their imagination, in both instances remaining open to the unexpected. But we can also see how other people can use only a narrow colony of objects. They either put their whole life into a single object of passion or, though endlessly discovering new objects, are unable to be nourished by their use.

I have been struggling with the urge to make ethical claims for the use of integral objects, but it goes without saying that at times we will all be obsessed, preoccupied, or passionate in our object relations. It is impossible to distinguish clearly among these three states of mind, but each, in its own way, restricts our freedom to use the object world. Although each requires our concentration, it differs from the kind of concentration often seen in a child whose intense energy is focused on *one thing*.

When the child discovers the *difference* between objects, a principle lies in wait: life offers many different objects, each of which can give to the self unique experiences and transformational possibilities. It is my view that these objects of desire are precisely what life has to offer. We call it "the spice of life." Variety. Difference. Uniqueness. To live life fully, the self must be open to its objects.

Intriguingly, once this principle is comprehended, then the self is free to use familiar objects in new ways, having in part discovered that the difference that comes with an object's structure supports the re-viewings generated by subjectivity. This is especially so with personal relations. John is married to Mary and lives, therefore, with a familiar other; each day, though, he experiences her differently, not because she is necessarily different, nor because he projects more of himself into her, but because he has internalized a principle of difference that informs all his object relations.

Much is made in the psychoanalytical literature of the differentiation between self and other or subject and object. Here I refer to another differentiation—between objects. Some persons, as we know, approach all things as if they were the same. The autistic child would seem to do this, so that along with his difficulty in differentiating self from other, he has an additional problem in distinguishing among the qualities of objects. The child's unconscious discovery of the integral object leads to his grasp of a principle—that life is to be used as an object—which in turn sponsors a certain sensibility in which the child (and later the adult) seeks things unconsciously, appreciating their experience potential. Because an adult seeks objects of desire, and his use of objects under the terms of this principle must be necessarily ruthless, he develops a profound gratitude toward life—for what it offers and for how it can be *taken*. Such an individual conveys not rapacity in the choice and use of objects but almost exactly the opposite: a kind of pleasure in being, a knowledge that there is sufficient experience to go around.

Interestingly, certain obsessive, preoccupied, and passionate uses of the object express an unconscious hatred of life as an object. By selecting one aspect of a life to which to devote the entire self, the individual expresses a form of self-mutilation through imposed restriction. A finger is unconsciously pointed toward the single object: "You see what my love of you has done to me!" Certainly here one can see the familiar reproach to life itself: "All these years I have been trying you, and look what I get in the end!"

A patient who was a passionate collector and restorer of old cars, to which he devoted all his time and energy, was virtually wiped out by the recession. In our sessions his recurring refrain, directed at life in general, was: "I don't know what I did wrong. All these years, what did I do? I worked. I worked and worked and worked. I knew more about Mercedeses and Rollses than anyone else in the world. I made scores of customers happy. And what do I get in return? This! That's what I get. And I tell you, I am fed up. Absolutely fed up!" In this transferential action the analyst is put in the place of life itself, in which he is presumably meant to reply on behalf of life as an object and say something intelligibly compensatory.

Life is not easy, as we all know, and when it gets difficult some may attack it. This is notably true in middle life, when people are most vulnerable to disillusions, so it is interesting to note how at this point some people seem suddenly to become passionately enlivened in relation to an object such as sailing or jogging. Of course, what one may be seeing is an apparent interest in life after a long period of no particularly intense investment. But it may also be an unconscious expression of the very hate I discussed above.

Some may say, surely this is better than withdrawal from

life? And I would agree. Strange as it might seem to support the therapeutic effect of hate, it is still a form of life to hate something passionately rather than to withdraw into isolation and indifference.

It is held as a virtual given that marriage, the raising of a family, the development and maintenance of a career are all signs of life. Psychotherapists and psychoanalysts will often point to one or all of the above as indications of progress during treatment. We are less comfortable looking at these standard choices in more realistic terms, which might reveal how these conventions sometimes become obsessions or preoccupations and are by no means necessarily *uses* of life. Marriage, family, and commitment to work inevitably narrow the individual's ability to use life as an object *even as* they enrich him. Although such paths deploy the self through the object world and are always profoundly meaningful, such conventions may become needless restrictions on the self, which may in turn remain undetected precisely because the conventions are so valued. Those esteemed Victorian ideals are often less life-enhancing than we think, even though, as Freud maintained, family serves to propagate the race and can therefore be seen as constitutive of the life instinct.

Take, for example, the mythic creatures of conventional man and conventional woman, those idealized figures who marry, raise children, develop their careers, perhaps have grandchildren, retire, and with luck are relatively disease-free and die at a respectable age. We know that the conventional partnerships all too often break down: marriages end, families fall apart, careers cause great anguish, and so forth. Still, the norm persists as the preferred option. But what if these conventions have become unconsciously insufferable restrictions on the use of life as an object? What if a conventional partner is not actually living his or her life, although performing the convention well? And, grotesque and unfair as it may seem, what if a divorced man, a family-opted-out woman, a career drop-out, or a maverick is an indicator of a move toward greater life usage?

When conventions are employed "conventionally," functioning as preoccupations rather than as real uses of life, we can see how object relations can lack that vital element that Winnicott referred to as ruthlessness. The infant, according to Winnicott, asserts the right to use the object ruthlessly (the mother in the first instance), and to create his own other. In so doing, he both enriches the inter-relating with his desire and appreciates the other's intrinsic value.

However, where a relationship is overly bound by convention, this right to ruthlessness may not be exercised, as the following example demonstrates. John and Mary are married and have three children. Jane—a friend of Mary's—invites her to a weekend in the country. Mary feels the pull of the possibility. A potential space opens up. Objects—out there—await. New things. Unseen. But Mary feels it would be wrong to leave John with the children, or even to leave the children for the weekend. So do the children, perhaps. And so too, very possibly, does John. Mary says, "Another time," and a lost opportunity goes the way of all inactivated futures: it is consigned to the ward of thwarted gestures, a unit that hospitalizes the crippled possibilities of life.

The example illustrates how Mary capitulated to the terms of her family relationships rather than asserting her right to occasional ruthlessness in the interest of self expression or her own life instinct (as opposed to the

Freudian view that the life instinct's function is to preserve the species). To use life as an object, each person must, in my view, engage in a critical deconstruction of the conventions of life that are supportive but not, ultimately, sustaining.

Odd as it may sound, the child raised in a setting where conventional assumptions about "family life" are never challenged may be psychically very restricted, since anything nonfamilial, hence strange or different, is excluded. Is it so very strange to say, then, that some of those ideals of lived life which we cherish so highly, such as a family, may be a restrictive psychic structure for the child if it exists fundamentally to the exclusion of the nonfamilial —i.e., the strange or the different? It may be the relatively rare family that builds into its structure a principle of deconstruction, in which the family understands its need to be displaced by the child's desire. In this sense we can see the Oedipal tragedy in a different light. Poor Laius and Oedipus were hitting the road for new adventures (i.e., different objects), but unlucky them, they collided with what they thought was strange but in the end it *still turned out to be family*. It may well be that this aspect of Sophocles' play objectifies a dilemma for all children (and parents): how to strike the correct balance between family commitment and personal articulation.

We may also wish to consider another dimension to the family romance, in which the child imagines himself to be the offspring of other parents. The notion that he or she is born of more illustrious parents not only may be an Oedipal expression of denigration of the actual parents (and all the other important psychoanalytic considerations that go into this concept) but sometimes may be a tacit expression that the family is indeed too restrictive, and thus give rise to the idea of a more generous family that would be willing to fulfill the child's desire.

The principle that life is an object to be used is also supported by the mother's native wisdom that infants thrive on the introduction of the new, or the continued reintroduction of the familiar re-created anew each time; but oddly enough, this is often consigned to the privilege of infancy and childhood and displaced in adulthood by Victorian notions of collective progress. Children's playing, their painting, their songs and linguistic inventions, are powerful indicators that well before school they are on the way to a creative invention of reality. Are we truly satisfied that our examination of social norms—our schooling and our family conventions—continues to serve such a creative evolution? Or are there times when we have unwittingly used convention as a thoughtless attack on creativity? Are there, for example, certain features of primary school education which foster unconscious hatred of life as an object through rigorous application of convention upon the child?

Intriguingly, it may well be that individuals sometimes develop obsessions, preoccupations, or passions as transformations of hate. Life becomes an object of hate because the self had to abandon object usage and idiom articulation much too early, setting up a developed envy of life. This envy—of the self that could have been but will not now be—can lead to a form of indifference, or a masochistic celebration of life's conventions that would appear to be evidence of adaptive creativity but that in truth is an attack on the self through a too vigorous embrace of the necessary devotions of a lifetime. Thus, finding a passionate interest in *one* phenomenon to the exclusion of all others can in certain circumstances be a compromise formation between total restriction and the freedom to develop. Hatred of life, in this instance, has been transformed into passion, now generated by more than a fair share of hate, but fortunately enough, it may become a transitional affect, leading the self to use of the object, to some liberating freedoms of idiom movement, and through this to a limited but meaningful love of life.

Freud viewed civilization as a human discontent because man and woman had to transform certain sexual and aggressive urges into an identification with a collective norm, thus seriously hampering the freedom of such impulses. Winnicott offered a somewhat different view: the child would, of necessity, become false in relation to his inner reality if he wanted to comply with the others' notion of acceptable action and if he wanted to get along in the group. Of course, Freud's vision offers us the example of those who are perverse and those who, through overidentification with the superego, take pleasure in the repression of libido and aggression. Winnicott's false self, who loves and identifies with convention, is not Freud's sadomasochistic man, but rather a creature who has transformed the idiomatic movements of the true self *into* the pleasures of the false self.

If we do not see the pleasures to be gained in many contemporary Western cultures for those who develop the false self, then I do not believe we can adequately understand a certain hatred of life that sets in much later. I am talking about a self that genuinely identifies with the dismantling of idiom and enjoys the culture of false self. *Enjoiners!*

What about the frustration that results from the adoption of a conventional self? If, as I maintain, there is an urge to articulate the unique form of the self through its choice and use of objects, what happens to that urge when the self abandons this desire for another?

Idiom and its articulation valorize difference. The pleasured journey of the false self valorizes convention. As many contemporary individuals exchange difference for sameness, *the loss of the urge to disseminate idiom is transformed into an unconscious hatred of difference.* Thus we can see that in a culture where convention is strongly emphasized, a profound unconscious hatred of difference can evolve. If we look for a moment at the United States, we can see that as it develops a sense of normative or conventional behavior—now termed "political correctness"—then idiom becomes hated. The gruesome paradox here is that politically correct behavior and its offshoots (e.g., multiculturalism) herald the rights of group difference but are part of a mentality that implicitly demands convention. Indeed, the very loss that many ethnic groups have experienced as they become Americanized is transformed into a form of hate. But it is arrived at not only through persecution from the outside but from the development of a false self within, which demands that the true self be abandoned for the life of the new conventional self.

One of the pleasures, then, of the false self—which enjoys its identifications and is well rewarded by the internal and external groups—is its disavowal of idiom and its destruction of the spontaneous gesture. Metapsychologically it is incorrect to describe this as an act of repression. As the idiom of the individual develops through its idiosyncratic use of an object, when the gesture behind the use is foreclosed, one does not get the repression of a content, but the eradication of this form of desire. What is the status, insofar as unconscious memory is concerned, of the eradicated?

There is a trace of the event and the net result is an inhibition of the expression of idiom. Inhibition—the opposite of exhibition—is the cumulative outcome of the eradication of one's difference. We come to another paradox. As the true self is inhibited, I think we often find in the ordinary exchange of things an extroversion of the false self. That is, as the person unconsciously forecloses the spontaneous gesture, he or she exchanges the loss of spontaneity for a gain in false-self exhibitionism. This is not exhibitionism in the ordinary psychoanalytic understanding of this action but an exhibition of the conventional self, a celebration of the false self as it embraces the normative. In contemporary culture this is visible in the celebration of fashion (in dress, phrases, behavior) which binds the individual into the group's celebration of commonality. Such celebration is not intrinsically problematic. It is pleasurable to be part of a group, and may be consistent with an idiomatic investment in the group, but the problem arises when convention is used to destroy the life of idiom.

Being bound to a convention and developing a false self that seeks adaptive joys is comprehensible if we bear in mind that individual subjectivity is intrinsically hazardous. As the self is disseminated through its engagements with objects, it becomes increasingly more complex, and by the time of the Oedipal complex the child is well aware, in my view, that he contains an internal world of very different and subtle self and object representations that boggle the mind. It is exceptionally difficult to continue on one's way after this realization, to follow one's own footsteps in multidirectional pathways, to tolerate the absence of neat cohesions of meaning.

(Back to Sophocles and another view. Oedipus and Laius wanted to hit the road and celebrate a different way of life, but unfortunately they capitulated and had to find family—journeying into the unknown was too perilous.)

It is understandable, then, that ~~each individual is tempted to cancel his own idiom~~ and seek refuge in conventional vestments. Although a person will, of course, be recurrently made aware of his idiomatic difference—through dreams, specific sexual desires, aesthetic choices—he will nonetheless embrace an order of things that carries the self through life on the tramways of convention and seek a false self that can stand in for the true self. But each person who does this may have to pay the price, in middle to late life, of not knowing what it would have been like to be oneself. Such individuals may feel very deeply angry about their condition.

To add to the overall unfairness of things, life lived more or less according to the unconscious dissemination of the subject's idiom is not so glorious. Complexity is hardly reassuring. The subject tries one thing and then another, operating by trial and error in much the same way as the scientist; and as with science too, there may be many hypotheses but little that is concrete. ~~But to articulate the self through the discovery and use of objects adds to the person's sense of inner reality and to the feel of life as something one has lived.~~

We know this to be the case with certain individuals, of whom it is said at news of their death, "Ah, but *what* a life he lived," this usually referring to their *jouissance*. A person like this has ~~used life as an object,~~ engaged people in deep friendships, encountered new phenomena, enriched others, and above all, perhaps, ~~*dared to be before he knew what it meant*~~. He was a "liver," she really "knew how to live," he "really lived life to its fullest," or she "never stopped realizing the wonder of life."

Perhaps most commonly, however, one hears that such

a person had "a love of life," and although some of this love will be the celebration of convention, we are in fact referring to the person's joy in being alive and in being a self. This is the person who uses life up but who enriches the object of use at the same time, and one who ultimately transforms convention.

5

The Functions of History

The psychoanalytical insistence on the priority of the imagined—juxtaposed, if necessary, to the happened—is understandable, if regrettable. Each person's inclination to describe his present state of mind as determined by external events is countered by the psychoanalytical perspective, which insists that such an account must be regarded in terms of the person's potential wishes or object-relational aims, even if it coincides with events which have, so to speak, happened.

Do we have to choose between the imagined and the happened? Are they opposed? The happened will always become part of the subject's imagined life—since perception of events is processed by the person's particular way of thinking and as time passes will become more subjective—but even if we take this into account, does this mean that the integrity of the actual loses status? To use Lacan's deposition from Kant: because we cannot truly grasp the real, does this mean that events in reality are left to our imagination? Lacan, however, ascribes powerful

influence to the real. It is there. It may evade representation but the fact is, reality happens to one, and there is
a kind of categorical memory of its nature. So, according
to Lacan, we do not remember the actual event that
happened to us, because our perception of reality is
disqualified by our own subjectivity—guided as it is by its
imaginative capacity and the latent rules of the symbolic
order—but we do recall the categorical moment, if one
can put it that way. We recall that something happened
from the real (not the imaginary or the symbolic) that
profoundly affected us.

Let us begin by thinking about some of the facts of life.
A patient tells us that when he was two years old a brother
was born. This is a fact. When he was four his family
moved from a small country town to a large city. That is
a fact. When he was six his grandfather died. That is a
fact.

Fact (from the Latin *facere*, to do; *fact-um*, "thing done")
first of all means "a thing done or performed," in the
neutral sense of action, deed, or course of conduct. But
the Oxford English Dictionary, interestingly, lists four
more usages of this first meaning of "fact," all now obsolete,
in which we can see a virtual history of the word: "a noble
or brave deed, an exploit," "an evil deed, a crime," "actual
guilt (as opposed to suspicions)," and "an action cognizable
or having an effect in law." So in the first place it is essential
to establish that certain events in a life are not just
imagined, that "thing" is "done." Notice how difficult it is
to get it right. "Thing done" is more accurate. It does not
say that someone has committed the action. Throwing a
spear at an antelope is a thing done, and a rock falling
from a cliff or a tree blocking a path is also a thing done.
Perhaps in the beginning of human consciousness it was

more important to establish that certain things got done, and it was less important whether they were caused by man or not. What mattered was that they were done.

A thing "performed," however, certainly suggests human authorship. We could say that the sea performs high waves or that the weather's performance is dramatic (and perhaps thousands of years ago we were willing to accord dramaturgy to the elements), but "a noble or brave deed" suggests human action, and epic narrative is constructed around brave deeds done by people. But the exploits are often attributed to mythic figures, and in the cases of actual persons (Jesus, for example) the deeds done are fantastical. It seems that the moment we enter the human arena, we lose our grip on the factual. A more modern understanding would be fact as evil deed or crime: "Do you promise to tell the whole truth and nothing but the truth?" Gradually it has become important to establish the facts of a matter, particularly when a crime has been committed and someone is guilty. It was, of course, the tradition from which Freud emerged; his hysterical patients suffered symptoms that upon elaboration suggested stories, and by transforming the symptom into its narrative, he confronted a problem: had these young women suffered some sexual abuse or were these fictions that expressed their frustrated desires? Freud never resolved this dilemma: the abuse could have happened, but equally, it might be invention. One of his discoveries, however, was that unconscious wishes could lead to the invention of a history, and he turned his attention to the motivations of self-deception, recognizing that one has to attend to the lie before one can ever reach the truth.

Freud's conception of the psychoanalyst, as a detective sifting through the clues that lie on the surface, privileges the fact, which, certainly by the end of the nineteenth century, was becoming more important in jurisprudence, too. In a way, the analyst was detective, counsel for the defense, public prosecutor, and jury all in one: areas of his mind were delegated to these various parts, while the different parts of the patient's self presented conflicting evidence.

We find ourselves now, at the end of the twentieth century, with a strange and disturbing revival of the question: what is fact and what is fantasy? Since the mid-1960s, when the Kempes' important work on child molestation in Colorado startled the American people, state legislatures and government regulatory agencies have passed laws and guidelines that in some cases mandate clinicians to report any allegation of child abuse (whether made by the child, by a friend, or by a neighbor). With such mandatory reporting, the patient's relation to a therapist is displaced by the patient's relation to the police. The details must be reported to the authorities, and a reported event becomes a potential fact; an investigative process is initiated, and the presence of the real overwhelms and displaces the possible valorizations of the imaginary or symbolic. The psychoanalyst is no more, at least as far as this patient is concerned, and the psychoanalysis cannot continue. We can see how the suggestion of a fact carries enormous power.

Matters are more complex, particularly in American culture, where the notion of abuse by the mother or father of a child has been widened from sexual abuse only to include physical abuse, emotional abuse, and abuses deriving from parental habits such as alcoholism. Victim support groups have formed around the objectified facts of such histories; and ascertaining what really happened to the person, sharing the "facts" of each member's life with the group, is now at the very heart of therapeutic recovery.

It might be viewed as comically ironic that psychoanalysis simultaneously is turning away from the value of history, removing itself from adjudicatory actions in relation to past facts, but the stakes are too high: more and more analysts are losing their right to consider their patients' internal worlds precisely because of a disinclination to take the factual past seriously, ultimately handing over this function to actual detectives! Indeed, with the emphasis on the concept of the here-and-now transference observation, a new and limited kind of fact-finding is being proposed: it is being suggested that we can pass judgment only on the clinical fact. And what is that? These are facts of performative action. How the patient treats the analyst as both an internal object and an actual other is observable over time and can be interpreted. The analysand is free to dispute these observations, although over the course of the analysis he may accept them. But the analyst will shy away from commenting on deeds done in the patient's life. It is claimed that this does not matter, since the facts that are truly pertinent to a psychoanalysis are those transpiring in the transference, and if things done to the patient in his or her childhood are true, they will be revealed in the transference which expresses the analysand's psychic life.

At the other extreme is an alarming Delphic therapy, occurring especially in the United States. Here is a typical example. A young woman who suffers anxiety is referred to a "therapist" for consultation. She is asked if she would mind going into a regression under hypnosis. She agrees to this, and upon recovering from her trance, the therapist solemnly tells her that she has been abused by someone in her early childhood, when she was about six. Who could it be? An uncle? A family friend? The therapist and the now deeply alarmed patient investigate figures from the patient's past. The patient is profoundly moved. Obviously an important truth has been uncovered, and it feels right—it must be right: but who was it? Sessions continue. Further regression therapies. And then a vague feeling, an awful and uncomfortable thought, banished in previous discussions with the therapist, can no longer be suppressed. The patient remembers that her father had a peculiar way of touching her. She cannot recall just what it was, only a memory of sensations, received from the hand of the father. The therapist deepens her voice. Pauses now seem minutes, before the verdict is read. The facts are beginning to assert themselves. The truth cannot be denied. Tears overwhelming her, the patient is led to the inescapable conclusion that she was sexually abused by her father. That she cannot recall the moment of abuse or any subsequent references the father might have made in relation to it does not matter. This, it is argued, is consistent with the nature of being abused. An event such as this erases memory. There are no memories. Absence of memory is the indictment. Any patient who has suffered a serious borderline disorganization of personality is now, finally, coming into an integration. For the first time in her life she not only feels she knows what is true and what is false but also feels she is coming together as a person. Now, as she develops intense and focused hate of the father and all that he stood for, as she tells her sisters, as she joins a victim support group, her life is given a definition it had never had. The proof is in the recovery. Therapy does not lie. With this oracular therapy, facts are declared. The thing done is found. The perpetrator of the deed is identified. A judicial process is enacted in the clinical situation. The criminal is tried in a family court and his reputation is destroyed. He is a new kind of vermin.

Psychoanalysis, some have argued, has deserved the fate it has received in some legislative quarters: neglecting the facts of a patient's life in favor of the more elite and arcane world of psychic events, it is no longer in a position to speak to the actual events of a patient's life. When it comes to matters of abusive deeds done, this is for the police, oracular therapies, and victim support groups. Even a cursory walk through a bookstore will indicate scores of self-help psychology books relating to recovery from abuse. Little will be found in the section on psychoanalysis.

But in psychoanalysis, is there a place for a new emphasis on deeds done in a patient's life? Certainly the analyst can allude to the significant facts of a patient's life even if he does not know their psychic rendering. So if a patient tells his analyst that his mother is a Puerto Rican Catholic and his father an Iranian Muslim, this may be of significance and now and then needs mention. It does not need interpretation—unless the clinician has some idea of its meaning—but it requires occasional utterance and allusive reference. If, as an adolescent, the patient moved from a large city school to a small village one, this fact too will need mention, even if the analyst has no personal investment in its significance. But why refer to these events if the analyst thinks that doing so dilutes the intensity of the transference?

This brings us to what we might think of as the power of the deed: the evocative presence of reference to the real in a psychoanalysis. By referring to deeds done the analyst touches the plane of reality even if he does not know what he reaches. By referring to the actual he brings it into the imaginary on its own terms. It enters the analysis not as an elaboration—although that may subsequently happen—but initially as a dumb thing: a fact. "Them's the facts." Dumb. "The simple fact is . . ." And herein lies one of the truths about facts. A deed done—a move, a death in the family, a car crash, the birth of a sibling, a bankruptcy—seizes the self. The imaginary and the symbolic are suspended—for a few days, for weeks, for months, sometimes for a lifetime—at least in the circle of potential elaborations that surround the fact.

What is the value of bringing simple facts into something as intelligent as a psychoanalysis? Because certain facts of a person's life are almost always intrinsically traumatic: many things done create momentary caesurae (blanks) within the self. By naming such facts the analyst brings the caesurae to the consulting room—these blanks are evoked, their emptiness is felt, and trauma enters the analytical space. Neither analyst nor patient will necessarily believe that these facts are in the least relevant, but in some respects that is the point. From the point of view of projective identification, we can say that the analyst's disinclination to discuss such events is his unconscious reception of the intrinsic nature of the dumb show: he feels the insignificance of trauma, feels emptied by the fact. It is not that it means nothing; it bears nothingness in it and feeling it to be insignificant *is* the outcome of trauma.

———

Is this surprising? Think of the historian's task. He is confronted by a series of facts. In 1594, Elizabeth is Queen of England. This is a fact. That same year Henry IV, newly crowned King of France, enters Paris. Fact. That year the Edict of St.-Germain-en-Laye grants the Huguenots freedom of worship. Fact. On the Austro-Hungarian border the Turks conquer the city of Raab. Fact. In May of that year, the theaters open again in London; Marlowe's *Edward II* is performed. Fact. Thomas Nashe's *The Unfortunate Traveller*, a picaresque novel, is published. Fact. Shakespeare's *The Two Gentlemen of Verona*, *Love's Labour's Lost*, and *Romeo and Juliet* are completed. Giordano Bruno is seized by the Vatican and imprisoned. Richard Hooker publishes Volumes 1–4 of his *Of the Laws of Ecclesiastical Polity*, Caravaggio paints *The Musical Party*, and Tintoretto dies. The first opera is written: *Dafne*, by Jacopo Peri. Galileo prints his Golden Rule. These are all facts. Set one against the other, they are rather dumb objects, aren't they? To be sure, the historian of the sixteenth century has numerous associations to each thing done because he has worked on these facts for a long time. Furthermore, we know now that these facts have proved to be noteworthy. They are worth remembering. With more difficulty I could have listed other facts of that time which would be less evocative: more dumb still!

These facts do not in themselves give the person who is only vaguely familiar with sixteenth-century history much to think about—at least not on first mention. But if each of these things done was discussed and talked about repeatedly over a long period of time and other facts were listed, then they would begin to take on a certain meaning. For the moment, however, I wish us to enjoy them as the creators of momentary blankness. Perhaps precisely because they are the deeds done, we are suddenly aware of their seriousness. Ironically, nothing much comes to mind.

Are we to conclude, therefore, that in addition to the caesura created in an individual's life by a done deed there is a second gap (perhaps an echo of the first) in which we do not know what to do with the narrated fact, even when it has nothing to do with us? Again we are rather struck dumb.

Why?

As I imagine it, when the real is presented—as a thing done to us, or as a narrated thing done—we do not as yet know how to think it. There is something unthinkable about such facts of life. Winnicott would argue that this moment's loss of thought is in fact necessary. He noticed that in his clinical work with infants they needed time to recover from a thing done: he would present the infant with a spatula, the infant would have a look at it—a new object and therefore a new fact of life—and then look away; if he tried to force this new fact upon the infant the child would become distressed and cry, but if the spatula was allowed to stay there, exist in all its initial dumbness, then the infant could return to it with interest and investigate. Winnicott's highly suggestive observation can be applied to many situations prevailing in a psycho-analysis, but I would like to focus on the analyst's relation to the patient's presentation of the facts of his or her life. When a patient informs me of the death of a parent, or of a trauma, I do not know what to think; rarely does anything come immediately to my mind: I need time and I suppose I need to look away for a moment. As I am suggesting, the presentation of the factual, the outcome of a deed done to oneself, is always somewhat traumatic.

Does trauma create its own potential space? In a way, yes. Shocked by the effect of a thing done, the subject may not know what to do with *it*. Such a caesura becomes the potential matrix of psychic elaboration, if the individual can return to the scene of the fact done and imagine it, perhaps again and again. Indeed, it may be that such facts nucleate into unconscious complexes, collecting other facts from life which increasingly gravitate into a particular mentality that derives from the *hit* of the fact. There are fact addicts: persons who seem to feel that only the facts of their lives, particularly those which have been disturbing, have essential qualities. Ironically, however, if the "fact addict" freely associates to the facts, rather than treasuring them as things in themselves, then their status as dumb and unremovable objects is cracked by the disseminative effect of thought itself. And the analyst's interpretation of the patient's psychic reality, one derived from these associations, is intrinsically detraumatizing, for it creates meaning where nothingness existed.

In my view, psychoanalysis errs if it turns away permanently from the presentation of the real, taking refuge either in a theory of narrative or in a misplaced empiricism, where the only facts recognized are those enacted in the transference. The analyst must return to the patient's presentation of his or her facts of life not because they bear some meta-truth in themselves that will displace the patient's projective constructions of an internal world, but because the patient is *entering the intrinsically traumatic in the process of analysis, unconsciously asking that the trauma of things done be addressed.* This can happen only if the analyst recurrently mentions those events in the patient's life that seem to restrict imaginative freedom. The psychic inertness of dumb facts is disproportionately heavy in relation to their conventional significance: an odd and compelling truth in its own right. When a patient tells me in the first consultation that his mother died when he was under three, I do not know what to make of it, and what disqualifies it from my ready imaginative response is its very significance. I am arrested by it. I do not want to give it meaning; that will have to come from the patient. This is the effect of the presentation of facts in analysis. Often the more profound the fact, the less significance it yields. Profound facts are wrapped in their own traumatic space, and the analyst cannot think about it yet, so the analyst's recurrent noting of them becomes a stage in *his* recovery from the trauma of fact presentation and, in turn, assists the analysand in his own imaginative elaboration of the fact. But facts must be returned to: facts bear the nature of the real, and as such seem to be forever elusive, saturated with the irony that they are less open to our validation of their significance than the purely invented.

The blank nothing created by trauma interrupts the fecund exploration of unconscious processes; it momentarily stops the cycle of condensation and dissemination that is intrinsic to an individual's unconscious elaboration of personal idiom. Indeed it provides an altogether different separate sense, the sense of one's development inside a structure imposed on the self rather than derived from it. The sense one develops from trauma is derived from the very precise facts of one's life—one's fateful moments—while the sense deriving from one's unconscious disseminations is part of one's destiny drive: the urge to elaborate and articulate the intelligence of form that constitutes any person's unique sensibility. Each of us has the possibility of evolving a separate sense derived from unconscious development of our idiom—akin to a skill that further enhances work of this kind—just as each of us may have this capability foreclosed by the repetitive intrusion of fateful events, which educate us in a different form of intuitive knowing: an unconscious talent for putting the self into traumatizing environments in which the self seems to operate with unusual skill.

———

Each person has a past, even if it is unclear quite what that "past" is. In the simplest possible sense, it is all that has preceded the present; hence it is by no means limited to a chronological sequence of happenings, but includes all mental happenings. Dream and actual event coexist in each person's past.

One of the more intriguing aspects of a psychoanalysis is that patients inevitably find themselves talking about their past, although the talk is not subjected to a rigorous ordering of sequential events, and more is excluded than included; it is always a selective recollection. In going over one's past, even when returning to the same epoch in one's life, new events or prior mental states are recollected, and the past becomes a kind of layering of narratives, each ordering the revival of the past in differing ways with different intentions.

We may ask how a person can contemplate his past: what variations might there be in such a consideration and what problems arise from such a reflective activity? All of this quite naturally relates when the analysand talks about his past in a psychoanalysis.

No one can talk fully about his past, any more than a historian can succinctly answer the question "What was the seventeenth century in England?" If the historian tries to answer the question in the abstract—that it was a transitional period from monarchical power to parliamentary democracy—this by no means does justice to all the facts of that time. No more, say, than if I were to state that from the age of nine to the age of twelve I was in transition from Pasadena to the coastal town of Laguna Beach. But in a way this is how we talk about the past when asked to objectify it thematically.

I have suggested that the past as a mental phenomenon is a sequela, in part, of dumb moments when the self was arrested by facts of life. Momentous events, markers in each person's life, are self-defining statements even though, as I maintain, not only do we not know what they mean but they also signify the power of nothingness. Equally, we live not only within the parochial world of our own unique family evolution, and the character of our own mental events (our dreams, erotic fantasies, daydreams, ideational preoccupations, and so forth), but also in a social world which naturally becomes part of our past. In 1967 I was in my final undergraduate year at the University of California at Berkeley. I worked as bibliographer for the history department during the day, and in the evening I managed a bookstore on Ghirardelli Square in San Francisco. I dated several women but continued to fancy one in particular. I was also having psychotherapy with a psychoanalyst at the student health service, gaining my first true experience of what psychoanalysis is. I can recall the flat where I lived, the car I drove, and later that year, the East Bay Activity Center, where I worked with autistic children. Pushed, I can recollect two or three of my favorite restaurants, recalling the Szechwan Chinese restaurants that became suddenly quite popular. I also played a lot of volleyball. And my antiwar activities continued. But "my past" that year must also include data beyond my own local interests.

In 1967 the United States and North Vietnam began peace talks in Paris. There were riots in America's black communities. Thurgood Marshall was the first black to be appointed to the Supreme Court. The Greek-Turkish war on Cyprus broke out. Norman Mailer published *Why Are We in Vietnam?*. The Beatles released *Sgt. Pepper's Lonely Hearts Club Band*, and Jean-Luc Godard's *Weekend* hit the cinemas. Christiaan Barnard performed the first heart transplant operation, the Boston Strangler was sentenced to life imprisonment, the astronauts Grissom, White, and Chaffee were killed in their space capsule, and Expo 67 opened in Montreal. These are a very few of the memorable events of 1967. They too are part of my past.

But is my concept of my past actually informed by these events? I am not at all sure. Of course, once I begin to think of specific things I was doing and what was going on in the world in 1967, I can begin to recall something of my being then. I could describe some of these details and also reflect on the world events and what they meant to me. But I do not think this is how we think when we consider the past.

The OED helps get me closer to what I think this word means. "Gone by in time," "lapsed," "done with," "over": first-order definitions bringing to mind the phrase "It's over with, in the past: forget about it!" So does the past signify a forgetting? When we think about the past, are we, in fact, directing our reluctant attention to something which is meant to be forgotten? Does this in part explain why it is so difficult to remember our past? Not because we cannot recollect it—we know very well that if we break it down into years, we can remember quite a few things —but perhaps because we are not meant to "delve into the past," to "awaken the past."

Does nostalgia, that curious pining about one's past, refer to a different kind of loss, the loss created from forgetting? Is mourning an act of riddance, which expels memory and displaces it with a here-and-now consciousness? If this is so, what does it mean?

The abuse movement, now giving birth to thousands of born-again victims, may hold a clue to the annihilation of discrete memories evoked in the word "past." As an oracular therapist listens to a patient's description of his past, a powerful organizing message is cohered. Something happened in the past, and that past event casts an entirely new light upon the present and simultaneously organizes the past into a narrative order that will explain everything (or nearly everything) to the subject. The vague sense that the past is a mystery is now gone. The feeling that something awful happened is proved correct.

Yet what if the past itself is the vague something that is awful? What if there is something intrinsically destructive of self about it? Would this not make all of us victims of some sort—direct victims of the past? "It is water under the bridge." "Let bygones be bygones." "It's history, man. Forget it!" A past that signifies forgetting, one that is very different from the Freudian theory of repression. The repressed, as opposed to the past, signifies the preserved: hidden away in the organized tensions of the unconscious, wishes and their memories are ceaselessly struggling to find some way into gratification in the present—desire refuses annihilation. But lived experience is shredded.

How can we conceptualize the past within psychoanalytic metapsychology? For what I am talking about is equivalent not to repression or denial, but to that amnesia which Freud writes about—the oblivion of *self* destruction, the eradication of all those fine and discrete details of a lived life that make each of us unique and unrepeatable, which sponsors a pining for what has been, a form of mourning deriving from a continuous intrapsychic process of self destruction.

Some might argue that it is simply impossible to remember one's past. There is so much detail—too much, in fact. We must forget in order to exist in the present. And in a way psychoanalysis supports this notion. Each session must begin with a blank screen. The prior session must not bias the analyst's open listening as he hears from his patient as if for the first time. Bion suggested that each analyst must dispense with memory and desire. In order to live in the present, we must, as it were, destroy the past. This makes some sense. Certainly we cannot "hold on to the past," or so we are told.

Much of psychoanalytic theory is concerned with loss—and loss of the object in particular. From Freud through Klein to Mahler, and throughout the literature, loss of the object is stressed again and again. We seem to have a thousand ways to lose it. Have we forgotten the loss of the self, its continuous destruction through consignment to oblivion? The ubiquity of nostalgia alerts us to the narcissistic issues relating to losses of one's past, losses that alter the self's history: the loss of one's youth, the loss of loved ones, the loss of "futures." When we speak of the past we conjure a signifier which identifies a self state that is almost appallingly obvious: we eradicate our lived experiences by forgetting them, turning discrete experiences laden with love and hate, turmoil and serene beauty, into a globular notion—the past. The term signifies the ultimate decay of finite lived experience.

Simply put, the *passing* of time is intrinsically traumatic.

———

I should like now to discuss a psychoanalytic patient whose relation to the facts of his past changed the course of his analysis.

Felix is an architect in his early thirties who emigrated from Hungary with his parents when he was three years old. His parents moved to Scotland, where they set up an agricultural business that did fairly well. They retired in 1979. Felix's father died in 1982 of a heart attack, and his mother died of cancer in 1987. Felix was their only child, but at the time of his mother's death his marriage of three years had produced two children, and when he began analysis he had three children.

In the first few weeks of his analysis he described his family's history in painstaking detail. When he was two and a half weeks old his mother developed an abscess on her breast and he was put onto a bottle. When Felix was a year and a half old his mother had acute appendicitis and was rushed to the hospital in the middle of the night. He told me this was his first memory. He could only recall being awakened, people bustling around the house, and an overall commotion that seemed very frightening. He is sure he remembers this, but cannot recall if the "memories" of asking for his mother and being told she wasn't there, or of other sorts of "askings" and "sayings," were revisionist. He vividly recalls the move at three, and he recalls that at four his father was crushed by agricultural equipment and had to be taken to the hospital. The mother's family moved to Scotland when his family did, and he remembers his age and what he felt like when each of them subsequently died. And of course there were other "facts" in his life.

My psychoanalytical bias informed me that some of these facts were likely to be quite important: the loss of the breast at two and a half weeks, the mother's hospitalization, the move, the father's accident. Felix's first years of analysis, however, were taken up with matters of the present. He was estranged from his wife, Alice, and although they lived together they were not on good terms: he found her clingy and dependent. He told me that he found "relationships" revolting, the very mention of the word causing his stomach to turn over. Unbeknownst to Alice, Felix had a sequence of lovers, from a week's "stand" to several months of intense fucking. He loved the "new-ness" of each sexual occasion, and found the very specific uniqueness of each woman's erotic requirement compelling. But whenever the woman began to depend on him or make demands on him, he could not bear this, and would very directly and often brutally break off the relationship and go to another lover.

When we discussed these affairs from several different analytical perspectives he refused them any potential meaning. They were simply good fucks, he valued erotic life very highly, and when *it* went, then unfortunately but necessarily his lover was jettisoned.

Among many considerations of these affairs I shall mention only two here. He would tell me in considerable detail what it was in the woman's way of lovemaking that he liked so much. It varied from one lover to the next. With X, for example, he found the way she sucked his lip and then nipped it at the end very exciting. She would also gently hold his testicles and then release them. She would climb onto his back and breathe into his ear from behind. He found instinctively that she liked to be licked under the arms, that when he put her hands on her pubic hair and pressed, while he kissed her ear, she had an orgasm. He learned that she liked to be lifted a few inches from the bed just before penetration. In time, as he increased his erotic knowledge he would look into her eyes, and she would look into his eyes, and this mutual gaze that recognized reciprocal erotic knowledge added enormously to his excitement, and made such encounters so blissful.

At a certain point I said that these love sessions were

like breast feeds; his insistence that such erotic quests were essential seemed rather like an infant claiming a ruthless right to the breast irrespective of the mother's personal requirements. When his lover became dependent upon him, she changed from an object for ruthless use into a person who demanded something of him and thus spoiled what they had created.

For years I put this interpretation to Felix, but he always denied its significance and refused any and all interpretations of his relationships. For example, when his women became dependent and then desperate—because he was rejecting them—I said that I thought he could not bear to come into contact with his own dependent feelings and could deal with that aspect of himself only by expressing contempt for such emotions. When I added, as I often did, that he could not allow his need for me to come into consciousness, and that he dealt with his affectionate and loving feelings for me with scathing dismissals, he would reply, "Well, you're a typical bourgeois moron who has lost his mind by having a family. You obviously think you're happy, but you don't know what true pleasure is."

Now and then he would ponder his past. His parents' Hungarian origin and his extended family were of interest to him, and he could look into the past, even while he was intolerant of events in the present. I learned that his parents had been compelled to marry because his mother was pregnant. He told me that his father often described the tension in their home in Buda, when the mother's father argued with him and treated him like shit. The mother was anxious and depressed, lapsing into tears and begging for her father's mercy.

On the basis of these "facts" I said that it seemed likely that his mother had been too anxious and distraught to breast-feed him, and that his conviction that relations were a disaster might have much to do with feeling that it was disastrous to be truly dependent on the mother, not only because she took her living presence from him but because she brought anxiety and despair to the feeding relation. "I know this will sound farfetched to you, but I want to say it in any event, as I think your present view that relations are disastrous occasions of osmotic contamination by the other's malignant need is a conviction based on experience."

One day Alice found out about one of Felix's affairs, then discovered a few more; he left her, and the marriage ended within a week. Alice was devastated and wanted to talk it over with him, but he was adamant: he would not tolerate her accusations, nor did he intend to bear her pain. Furthermore, she was to blame: she had misled herself all along in thinking that a marital relationship could be permanent and he had never promised this. As she became more distraught and in her desperation acted out socially, he became more and more contemptuous of her, adducing her behavior as proof that he was right all along to consider relationships a disaster. "She is trying to make me feel guilty—as are you—and you can all go fuck yourselves with your own guilt, because *I do not* feel guilty. She is a sick woman and you are a bourgeois analyst with pathetic moral values of your own. While you just sit in your chair never moving all day, I am out and about, fucking some of the most beautiful women in London and enjoying myself. So don't you dare try to lay a guilt trip on me: I won't have it!"

In fact he was visibly shaken and vulnerable during such tempests. I would wait until he had calmed down (usually within the hour) and would then say that I thought

his guilt was unbearable, too painful, and he was desperate
that it be in his wife, or in me, but not in him. Sometimes
I would say that he had to denigrate me, to insist that his
way of thinking was the only way to think, lest he be
swamped by powerful emotions which he was certain
would overwhelm him. On rare occasions I would refer
to his mother's withdrawal of her breast, saying something
like "I think you are afraid that if you allow your feelings
to emerge, your feelings will be overwhelmed with your
mother's feelings of grief and anxiety, that you will lose
yourself unless you say *none* of this matters." Referring to
Alice—or one of his abandoned lovers—I would say that
he evoked a hunger in them akin to his own desperate
need as an infant, which had been ruptured by his mother,
and that his confusion was between the power of his own
emotions and the presence of his own mother's anguish.
I was careful to pick the correct moment to make these
comments. I had no expectation that they would prove
mutative in that moment. I constructed a history for him,
by linking past facts to present events only very rarely,
but I did so in order to give him the frame for a potential
act of eventual significance. Otherwise I stuck to the here
and now of his feelings, his transference relation to me
and the material he brought to the sessions.

A few years passed during which he became increasingly
available for insight into himself. He could now talk about
guilt and when he experienced it; he did not projectively
identify it into others. He was able to bear transference
interpretations and to discuss his feelings about me, including homosexual anxieties and primitive states of need
and anxiety.

Then Felix met a woman named Angela, and they were
soon involved in a passionate erotic relationship, only

this time, after some months, Angela tired of Felix and dumped him. This had happened to him once before but not to such devastating effect. A friend of Angela's— Fran—took Felix into her arms to give him solace. For a while he was comforted by this, but then the relationship became quite eroticized, and soon they were enamored of each other. Fran's true boyfriend returned from a year's sabbatical (trying to "find himself" in an Asian country) and after relatively little angst, Fran gave Felix his walking papers. It took months for him to recover, and while still in the midst of his grief he met Juliet at a convention of architects.

He had seen Juliet before, but only now did he find her exciting. To make a very long affair shorter, they fell into a mad kind of erotically mesmerizing love affair. The fact that Felix lived in London and Juliet in Scotland did not seem to matter: absence made more than the heart grow fonder. He would fly to Glasgow, she to London, and in airport lounges they would embrace with such passion that on one occasion airport security asked them to leave. Juliet adored him. She admired his work, which had brought him international acclaim. Now and then she would attend his "site visits" and be truly astonished by his capability; indeed, she learned from him, and he was quite pleased when eventually she won a major project for herself in Wales.

They usually spent weekends together, and between projects would live in his London flat. They made love several times a day. Sometimes they stayed in bed for virtually the entire day, making love and falling asleep, then making love again and having a bite to eat, then falling asleep, then having a bath together and giving one another a massage, then making love again, and then falling asleep. By this time in his analysis he knew there was something particular and meaningful about these particular love relationships. Whereas before, he would tell me about his sexual life in a contemptuous and exhibitionistic manner (with unconsciously homosexual libido operating in the transference), now he reported what was taking place because he knew there was something rather odd about it.

He had been shaken by Angela's and Fran's desertions. He came into contact with that part of him which he realized I had always been talking about—his dependent and vulnerable self—and fear of desertion was now in the forefront of his mind.

Juliet's success in Wales was nothing short of sensational. She was featured in one of the major international architectural journals, voted the outstanding architect of the year in another, and offered one job after the other. She enlarged her office, hired staff, and began to collect frequent-flier miles from her trips to other countries. At first Felix joined in the celebrations, but gradually he felt that Juliet held him in contempt: he was now less well known than she was. Clearly there had been a redistribution of power in the relationship. More disturbing, he discovered purely by chance that she had had an affair with another man. He was devastated, but after long conversations with Juliet and what appeared to be genuine remorse on her part he decided it was in his best interests to trust her.

In the sessions he would still talk about their love life and its particularities, but from an increased distance, in that now he knew what I meant by "erotic knowledge": he felt he knew her in a way he had never known anyone before and she knew him in a way that he had never been known. It was beyond words. Instinctive. Blissful. He tolerated my increasing use of the "breast" as a metaphor: yes, he agreed, it was possible that he was now, as I put it, at the breast, feeling that Juliet-mother had an instinctive knowledge of him and that he had an instinctive knowledge of her.

Months passed. Juliet would come and go. On two occasions I had an uncomfortable feeling. She told him first that she was going to meet a client in Singapore but then that plans had changed and they met in Tokyo instead. I did not give it much thought, but I felt uneasy. Felix was distressed by its being harder and harder to keep up with where she was going. Then she was to attend an awards ceremony in Stockholm, and he asked her to get a room for both of them, as he would join her. She said that would be fine, but a week or two later mentioned that it now looked like a purely working convention, and asked whether he was sure he wanted to come. As it happened, his plans had changed and he accepted the fact that he would not come. I felt a kind of force, as if she were pushing him away. I also sensed that she was lying.

Then catastrophe struck. Summoned to Rome to consult on a colleague's project, Juliet left Felix after a weekend's bliss in London. Felix's phone rang. With astonishing parapraxal skill, Juliet blurted out, "Gerald, where the hell are you!" Dumbstruck, Felix lapsed into immediate and intense silence. He knew it was Juliet, he knew she was phoning someone called Gerald; he knew she was in the midst of a mis-calling. "For God's sake, I'm sitting here in this stinking Roman hotel, waiting for you, you aren't here, you are there, I can hear you, and I'm fucking fed up with this," whereupon she hung up.

Felix's soul left his body. He walked around the flat not knowing what to do. He lay on the floor and did deep-breathing exercises. A botanist in his undergraduate life, he now watered his plants and talked to them in an empty voice. Finally he picked up the phone some thirty minutes later and rang Juliet in Rome. She was abrupt when answering the phone and he asked why. She said she was just overworked and a bit tired. How was he? Fine, he said. In fact, he said (lying a bit), he had booked a flight on the afternoon plane to Rome and would be with her that evening. When? she asked. Around eight, he said. Oh why, love, she implored, it's not necessary, I'll be back in London on Monday. No, he replied, he wanted to see her: he was coming.

That evening Felix was with her in her hotel when flowers from Gerald—a dozen red roses—arrived with a note attached saying his flight had been canceled, please forgive him, he would see her in a fortnight. For hours on end Juliet denied there was anything other than the purely innocent in all of this, but the more she talked, the more Felix could see chinks in her story. They talked through the night, and they made love several times. The next day, as they walked together along the Tiber, Felix managed to piece together certain *facts* she told him, enough finally to show that she had after all been lying. Put into that corner, she admitted it. She then laughed, said, "Poor love," slapped him across the face, and disappeared in the crowd. Dumbstruck, Felix sat on a bench for several hours. When he returned to the hotel she had gone. He dashed to the airport hoping to meet her, knowing in his guts that the relationship was all over but nonetheless hoping they could at the very least end the affair in some decent manner. But she was not there.

Odd as it may sound but perhaps understandably, given their intense erotic investment in one another, they had no mutual friends. There was no one he could turn to to ask about her. She had vanished. Phone calls to her office were met with icy responses. Married to his absolute desolation was the extraordinary fact of her complete and irremediable absence.

Felix had a breakdown. He could not eat. He was unable to sleep for more than a few hours at a time. He would wake up in the night, sit bolt upright, and "see her." He could not stop thinking about her. Every thought brought with it the pain of a feeling. An image would come to mind and with it whatever feeling it carried in its belly. He saw a hotel in Cornwall. It was where they had spent a lovely weekend, going for a walk along the sea cliffs, when she told him about her father's early death, and he was deeply moved. All the feelings of that moment returned in full force . . . and then, the awful pain that always followed: her absence. An image of the hotel in Rome came to mind and he was suffused with pain and anguish, and then the fact of her absence demolished that moment's emotion.

During this deeply anguished time in his life, Felix turned to the catastrophe in his recent past and painstakingly reconstructed the events leading up to the weekend in Rome, an hour-by-hour deconstruction of what took place in Rome, and as he did so, every few days he would "recover" a lost fact. He had forgotten. When she picked him up at the airport she did not give him the yellow rose which she always handed him. The hotel manager had said upon his arrival: "Ah, signore, glad to see you!" How did he know to expect him?

Session after session after session was taken up with his

recollection of a single fact, or two or three. He remembered that two months before the catastrophe, while cleaning out the car, he had found a hotel bill that had slipped from her pocket and thought it unusually high. He recalled that six weeks before, he was on the phone to Juliet's secretary when he believed her to be in Wales, and heard the secretary call out Juliet's name ("Juliet, can you sign this for me?"); he had not asked about what he had heard. He recalled phoning Wales sometime later and talking to the project manager of one of her enterprises. He said she was staying at the Red Lion Hotel, whereas she had told Felix she was staying at the Boar's Head Inn.

And Gerald. Who was Gerald? He did not know. But not a session went by without his trying to figure out who Gerald was. One theory yielded another. His sense of humor delivered the necessary transference interpretations: "I know, *you* are Gerald. What were you doing with Juliet!" The true significance of this link fell into a certain kind of place but did not displace the pain or the yearning.

The recovery of facts seemed a kind of lifeline. Each fact pieced him together as he tried to recover from his trauma.

Interpretative work at this level—of patient breakdown—is crucial. Felix was available for comprehension of himself as never before. For years he had rightly said that something was missing in his analysis, some essential truth. I felt we were amidst that truth, and I told him so. I said that I thought that he had unconsciously picked Juliet—as he had Angela and Fran—because there was a destructive element in her. With Juliet it seemed clear that she seduced him in order to conquer: once she achieved fame, he became the object of her contempt. His eventual dependence on her was his disaster. I said he had created this disaster with his female lovers prior to this, leaving them in his wake, but now here he was, with that wonderful breast that knew him and that he knew, and it suddenly vanished, taking his soul with it.

As he gradually put together evidence of Juliet's "other" self, a troubling discovery ensued. She was an accomplished liar and had cheated on him and, he was to discover later, other men before; but his negative hallucination of this fact, I maintained, was akin to his saying that the bottle mother was the true mother: he had to deny what he saw in reality in order to maintain a delusion of continued maternal presence. This interpretation and its repetition released a flurry of rediscovered facts which illustrated his capacity for negative hallucination. For example, he finally realized who Gerald was, and he remembered a parcel in her Edinburgh office with a label saying "From Gerald" with no return address. In fact, he had kidded her about it. "Who is this Gerald?" he had asked. And she had laughed and said, "Oh, one of my lovers, you idiot!" Then he recalled that the label was somewhere in his flat! They had traveled from Scotland in his car that day; they had scooped up all the belongings, including the parcel, put them in his car, and brought all the stuff into his place; Juliet had taken the parcel but for some reason had left the label. So where was it? After hours of searching he found it.

What he did then was of interest. He would stare at it, in disbelief, saying to himself, "I cannot believe this is true." Then an hour later, he would get the feeling that indeed *it was not true* and he would feel that he had imagined the entire episode. So he would return to the label and reread the name. In his mad state of mind he did this hundreds of times over a number of weeks, although the investment in the act gradually reduced over time until it became ordinary. He brought the label to show me, and he now talked openly about how he had been negating facts all his life: new memories from his early childhood returned.

For the first time he used my reconstruction of his relation to his mother in a meaningful way. He knew the truth that had been missing from his knowledge of himself: the fact of his dependence on her and his determination in life never to become dependent again meaning that the loving and needy part of him was relocated into others. But the awful ache, the terrible psychic pain of losing Juliet, this registered a terrible loss of a different kind. He created an *elisionary moment*, saying, "I have lost . . . I have lost . . ." and I said "everything," and in that moment he felt deeply known. We also knew that what he had unconsciously created with Juliet—although it started more actively with the other two women—was the scene of his own internal catastrophe. I said that I thought that however awful this experience was, it had constituted an enactment from the analysis; he had gone in search of a certain truth missing from the analysis and now he had found it.

For weeks he complained with great confusion about his state of mind. Repeatedly I said that for him it was a catastrophe *to feel*, and that having spent a lifetime being out of touch and not feeling, he regarded the arrival of his feelings as a disaster. It was, I suggested, his psychological birth, from the nonhuman to the human. This made sense to him, although it did not alleviate his pain. But the intention of psychoanalysis, as I told him, was not to alleviate this pain, as it could not, but only to indicate how it was ordinary, however awful, and to be expected.

Working with him during this time, I felt as if I were working with an infant who could talk, and who spoke with enormous surprise and protest about his feelings. For a while he resented Juliet's supposed freedom. He wished he could be like her and walk away and I said that he no doubt did miss the "smooth" parts of himself— those aspects that never felt anything for anyone—but now he was well and truly born, and there was no escape from his own psychic development.

Felix's relation to facts is of interest to our understanding of the individual's relation to his past and to our subsequent understanding of the function of history. A significant factor in his breakdown and recovery was his extraordinary devotion to finding out facts, yet each discovery bore with it the blank effects of deeds done. He was recovering trauma through the recollection of each and every fact of Juliet's abandonment. Since he had not been psychically present during his past (he had lived through instinctual ruthlessness and negative hallucination) not only were the facts of his life lost upon him, but their traumatic dimension was almost always passed to the other—usually the women he cast aside—who bore the dumb effect of events within themselves. Recovering these things done was his way of bringing trauma into the consulting room and working it through. His past would not, then, become an agglomerative signifier of profound personal injury.

Felix's preoccupation with fact illustrates one function of fact-finding in psychoanalysis, although most analysands are quite distanced from the important past facts of their life, as he was not. Because Felix had unconsciously reconstructed his past through a traumatizing set of circumstances in his present life, these present-day events were of extreme interest to him. He relived much of the trauma of his early infancy in the relation to Juliet, and the facts of that relation—what actually happened, as opposed to what he imagined or denied had happened—became quite pertinent. The unearthing of any single fact was not so remarkable in itself, but the process was essential; some of the facts—or things done—had been repressed or denied in the first place, so when he recovered the history of deeds done he regained contact with parts of himself that had been lost in acts of negative hallucination: quite literally, fact-finding became self-finding, even before the self could feel integrated.

Some of the recovered facts had been lost through forgetting; others through repression. Felix's disposition to rid himself of any contact with trauma—whether that of the unwanted idea or simply the suffering of things done in the first place—meant that he made no generative psychic differentiation between the repudiated and the forgotten. As facts of all kinds emerged in a proliferation of recollectings, he came to understand certain events as objects of repression, others as objects of denial, and most as simple facts from lived experience that bore the self state of their moment.

————

When we refer to "the past" we agglomerate the fine details of lived experience under a word that signifies the eradication of the self. The past is a cemeterial concept. Not only a burial ground of that which was enjoyed and cannot be recovered, of the many prior selves lived that are now lost to their former moments, but a term which eradicates the truth of the lived present.

Indeed, historical markers in a person's life—occasions that seem to be of self-defining significance—impose themselves upon the subject as his historical content. The characters, events, and choices of the past, when narrated, would seem to bear a heavy weight. But psychoanalysis and contemporary historiography suggest to me a rather different way of approaching the past and constructing a history.

Psychoanalysis pays careful attention to what it terms screen memories. These memories are usually not about highly significant events. Indeed they have a kind of Wordsworthian simplicity: the more discrete and detailed the memory, the more laden it is with significance. One thinks here of Proust's sense that the memory of a side panel at Combray contained within it more of his being in that moment, a discrete recollection of the people and the events at the time.

Freud said that a screen memory was unusually vivid and apparently insignificant. Readers may see the link between his concepts of the screen memory and my earlier arguments about experiences of psychic intensity. Screen memories are condensations of psychically intense experience in a simple object: the evocativeness of the commonplace. In *Forces of Destiny* (1989) I suggested that each of us contains historical sets, which congregate memories of simple events during the various epochs of our childhood; these screen memories bear the history of self experience, and insofar as they are often made up of displaced desire and trauma, they inevitably contain the essence of the more profound moments of our lives.

But when a person talks about his past, are these the events he describes? Almost certainly not. If given ten minutes, or half an hour, or even two hours, to tell another about one's own "case history," then the person will usually start with where he was born and raised, who his parents were, what events occurred in his childhood and adolescence, where he was educated, what interested him, what hobbies or sports he engaged in, and so forth. Since life affords us hundreds if not thousands of possibilities to create such historical narratives, after a while the person will even become rather practiced in them. Psychiatry certainly places great value on the "case history" narrative. A typical "case presentation" begins with the analyst recounting the histories of the individual's grandparents, then proceeds painstakingly through the history of the patient's entire childhood, diligently reporting the history of his sexuality, the history of his personal relations, the history of his education, the history of his family, and many other subhistories. The presenting clinician may then eventually work his way to the present, giving a history of the analysis up to the present time, by which time more than a few of those present may have nodded off or long since departed into private mundane mental preoccupations: what to buy for dinner that night, where to go for the weekend. However, when the clinician gets to the presentation of clinical material in the form of a process recording of an actual session or two, the atmosphere changes strikingly, and all but the senile are alert and concentrated, to hear—at last—*from the patient.*

I have rarely heard a case presented in this manner when I have not been surprised at the difference between the patient as a narrated historical object and the patient as a narrated presence in the session. Years back I would listen to the sessional material linking the prior details with the present report. This is not difficult and one need not be a psychoanalyst to make such links. But if one remains true to the difference, then often the analyst is left wondering exactly what, *if anything*, that historical narrative has to do with the nature of this person's being.

We come then to a strange paradox. The analyst's and analysand's report of his or her history is so often rather deadening, even though it is informative and theoretically enriching to the listener, while a session, even the mundane report of the patient's seemingly far less interesting parochial interests, is more intriguing. This paradox captures an important truth, which requires considerable thought on our part: the act of case presentation contains the eradications of the self, not the life of the self. This eradication is nullifying, and the sense of destruction is contained in the act of case reporting. Only when the present process session is reported does the case truly come to life. How do we reconcile this judgment with our placing value on the subject's history, on believing it to be crucial in gaining those limited truths in any person's memory of his being?

_____

In an interesting way a historian has *to forget* narratives of the past, particularly those written by other historians. Although they are of some interest, part of the history of history, they get in the way. Nor, indeed, can the historian content himself with the significant moments of history as things in themselves. The names, deeds, and deaths of great monarchs or historical figures may be common knowledge, and the historian will refer to such facts, but he looks elsewhere.

Migrating from one great library to another, or to small libraries that house particular archives, the historian reads the *minutiae*. Even an intellectual historian writing a work of considerable scope, sweeping across centuries, still buries himself again in the texts, going to a familiar psychic place he knows well, one of great solitude.

For historians who become psychoanalysts, the analyst's daily work and the life of the historian do not occupy the same psychic space, but there is a sense of similarity. Evenly hovering attentiveness and that scholarly attitude the reader takes while quietly perusing a text are not so different. With both, the ordinary work of gathering material and considering and reconsidering it over a long time yields true insights. In *Being a Character* (1992) I described the nature of unconscious work in which artists, scientists, and, one might add, historians organize data into constellations that nucleate into as yet unconscious new perceptions; these eventually break out into consciousness and become new ways of looking at phenomena.

The psychoanalyst who listens to his patient's history will often learn far more about the patient's past when, and if, the analysand simply recollects very small incidents. Here the "recovering of lost memories," the reemergence of the previously amnesial—not only the repressed but the forgotten—becomes rich material for history, as the patient describes one event after another in minute detail.

Proust had the right idea. As did Felix. To find one's history, the past, signifying the destruction of lived experience, must be displaced. The individual must be free to wander in and out of recovered memories, in particular those which are seemingly trivial. This exceptionally crucial act warrants emphasis, as many analysands are unsure whether such rememberings are "appropriate" for analysis. Of course, this breaks the golden rule that each patient should narrate any thoughts, but some analysts are inclined to regard the reporting of such facts as deviations from the here-and-now transference. These rememberings may be regarded, instead, as forms of splitting, in which the emotional intensity of the transference is displaced and

projected into the recollections, and some patients, knowing this or having heard of it, will be reluctant to waste
the analyst's time with such detail.

Naturally there are also neurotic reasons for these
inhibitions. For as Freud said of the screen memory, the
small details of a scene bear the most powerful wishes and
anxieties, and a patient may resist speaking of these rather
"secret" and sometimes "embarrassing" details; they are
embarrassing in part because of precise unconscious contents, and the *detailing* in itself seems to be embarrassing
—something historians recognize only too well. Asked
what he has been researching over the past few months,
the historian may feel embarrassed to disclose that he has
been reading the purchasing records of several houses,
the church, and other institutions in a small village,
studying how much corn was bought, firewood stored, salt
beef laid down, and the like. Why this embarrassment?

Freud's theory seems correct. The historian knows—
unconsciously—that work of this kind is devoted to gaining
the most profound secrets of an age. The scopophilic
guilt, the voyeuristic anxiety, all these are part of his
embarrassment as he knows only too well exactly how to
investigate the past. And so too with the analysand. Each
patient knows that he is engaging in a kind of introspective
scopophilia, the speaking of which becomes then an act
of preconscious exhibitionism. And for the psychoanalyst,
in the countertransference, there will have to be an internal
working-through of a similar sense: that to hear the
patient's secrets condensed into trivial memories is to pry
into the unconscious life of the other.

The shyness of the historian or the odd feeling in the
analyst who does not intervene when the analysand dwells,
perhaps for a long time, on very small details from the

past is understandable if we remember that this kind of work surreptitiously defeats trauma and revives the selves that had been consigned to oblivion. As Freud has taught us, nothing is lost on the unconscious. Recollection of small details is a kind of screen function within the self, as the small memory evokes the self state that prevailed at the time: remembering the small episodes of life revives selves from the past, even if the past as a totality remains chained to its dumb facts and reveals comparatively little.

The function of history in a psychoanalysis is most curious. Like the historian laboring away in his fields of examination, the psychoanalyst attends to fine details, because in them the self is recuperated through its screen memories. The momentous facts of life, or the dramatic things done, are the entrance of the real into the life of the subject—creating a momentary caesura, or blankness —and they stand in isolation, as markers of the subject's history, notations of trauma and subjective absence. They tell nothing, or tell of the presence of nothing. It is only in the displaced mentation of the subject, in his asides, his sotto voce mumblings—in the details of the seeming trivia of his life—that one can discover the true response to the deeds done.

History becomes, then, a life instinctual activity: it forges links with *le vécu* and mitigates the death work of certain facts. Many contemporary historians will deconstruct their conclusions or aim to do so. No historian, or historically minded psychoanalyst, can expurgate his desire: his wish *will be* to make certain conclusive statements. But such realizations do not testify to the function of history, which has already taken place, in the endless action of immersion in the material, there to be available for recognition of significance laid down in memory. These details, recovered from ordinary oblivion, gather a certain psychic force to them and provide psychic material for new insights.

The psychoanalyst who understands the function of history will recognize the enlivening and informative value of reporting small details: these displaced facts—some of which are constructed from the imaginary out of the traumatic effects of the real—are the intensities of a lifetime, and history is the recovery of such moments. It is as if the trauma of time passing is unconsciously managed by screen memories, which become underground wells in the deserts of time. Once tapped, these sources liberate private experiences and unconscious associations that prevailed in the past, and what was partially erased by the trauma of passing time is restored through free association to screen memory.

An extension of the concept of unconscious dissemination would therefore have to include the function of history making. By immersing himself in his texts the historian, like the analyst lost in the patient's production of material, is *temporarily deconstructed* by the multiplicity of his own findings and his unconscious elaborations of those materials. (I prefer to use the psychoanalytic word "material" to designate that which might otherwise be called data or facts, in that material also includes the nonfactual truth or the telling lie.) Each time a historian approaches his material or the analyst listens to his patient, his prejudices are *destroyed* by the action of reading or listening. Each also taps the screen memories of the other; the clinician directs the patient to liberate himself from the bleakness of ordinary trauma—the deserts of time gone by—to gain access to unconscious meaning stored all the while in the secret subterranean source of the screen memory.

Of course, both historian and psychoanalyst will have powerful beliefs, essential when the material is transformed by interpretation; this labor of consciousness is not only necessary but essential, an oscillation between one's beliefs and their existential deconstruction. The work of the unconscious not only destroys the manifest texts but fragments and scatters the views of consciousness. When there are points of convergence—between unconscious trains of thought, or between preconscious alertness and unconscious movement—then consciousness once again forms its interpretation. Good historians and analysts must be prepared for their own *undoing* each time they return to the material. For however biased they are, and however pleasurable it is to discover that one's views are correct, they should have another kind of desire, based on a separate sense, in which they take pleasure in the deconstruction of subjectivity, as they are resituated by encounter with their objects. They may be initially reluctant to allow for the implications of this deconstruction, but if they value the work of the unconscious, then they will find pleasure in this dismantling of self.

The function of history, then, is twofold. The historian-psychoanalyst brings his convictions to the analytical scene, where he listens to his patient sorting the material into convicted places, and he can then think about the patient according to his own ideological stance. But the very pleasure of seeking to be confirmed is destroyed by the analytical process, which breaks up unities and decenters the listening experience. Historian and psychoanalyst are experienced in the discovery of things done in the past. They know how to find hidden details, but once they are brought into the light of day, these details, although of course subject to interpretation, are too polysemous to stay in any one subjectivity's perspective. The discoveries —when true ones—displace the finder.

Historical thinking is a psychic function. Reviewing the past, retrieving finite details from it and giving them new, indeed contemporary, meanings, detraumatizes the subject who suffers from the ailments of many a thing done. By making past events meaningful, the historian exercises an important psychic capacity, that of reflection: this does not confer retrospective truth on the past—indeed, almost the contrary—but creates a new meaning that did not exist before, one that could not exist were it not based on past events and did it not transform them into a tapestry holding them in a new place. That new place—in history proper the text of the historian, in a psychoanalysis the series of reconstructions—is a psychic act: the work of the imaginary and the symbolic *upon* the real, creating a space in the mind that gives special significance to the real, transformed yet distinctly held, a space that for some people will always offer a kind of itemization of events which they understand to be the past. This movement of the real upon the self has the effect of giving the self the feel of its own many deaths; but in a psychoanalysis this past, transformed into a history, gives the real a place that is open to the continuously transformative workings of the imaginary and symbolic, the very movement that Freud termed *nachträglichkeit*, translated into English as "deferred action" or into French as *après coup*. This "revision" of the past, which suggests that the memories of the analysand are open to continuous revision subject to his contemporary perspectives, does not, as some would have it, invalidate the idea of reconstruction: it is simply the ordinary work of any historical activity. The past is inert. The dumb facts of an existence still lie in their chronological place, weighing heavily upon personal development. Doing history, however—reviewing this past and thereby transforming it—is a psychic function always alive to changed ways of seeing the world that will occur in the patient. Each person's past is open to continuous acts of historicizing, but again, this should not lead to skepticism about the worth of history making but, on the contrary, should inspire renewed recognition of the creative function of our psychological capacity to see the course of a life in continually new ways.

Alongside the dumb fact of a lifetime's "significant" events—which give the self its sense of trauma—are thousands of screen memories which also contain the history of the subject. Recovering the screen memories, or converting the dumb facts into projective screens for imaginative reliving, the psychoanalyst sides with the unconscious in its disseminative deployment of the subject's idiom, which has oftentimes been stopped and held captive by trauma. By transforming the past into a history, the psychoanalyst creates a series of densely symbolic stories that will serve as ever-present dream material in the patient's life, generating constant and continuous associations.

Unlike the past, which as a signifier sits in the self as a kind of lead weight, history requires work, and when the work is done the history is sufficiently polysemous to energize many unconscious elaborations. The work of recollecting seemingly insignificant details from the past symbolically brings prior selves contained in these mnemic objects back to life—and in this way transforms debris into meaningful presence—and thus is the work of a life instinct, but ironically it also puts these past lives into a new place of destruction, for the unconscious work has a dismantling effect, as historical texts of reconstruction give birth to other ideas and contrary reflective theories, which destroy the placid aim of creating commemorative plaques to one's new discoveries. Historical construction collects in order to retrieve the self from its many meaningless deaths—the amnesial "gone"—and then it generatively destroys these details and saturates them with new meaning created through the very act of retrieval, which has given them the imaginative and symbolic energy to make this past available for the self's future.

6

What Is This Thing Called Self?

Although we know what we mean by a self representation or an object representation, what do we mean by the self? Is it the sum of internal representations? We refer to *the self* as an object of an internal dialogue—one talks to one's self, for example—which suggests another. But we also define shifting states of self, particularly in emotional experiences, so do we include such shifting states in our notion of the self? And can there be a self state and a relationship to the self at the same time?

Waving goodbye to relatives from a ship that is about to depart, one might be sad thinking of those one is leaving behind, aware of a loss of part of one's self. A person flying away on a business trip may be anxious about the work to be done or perhaps about flying; his self and object representations may be intermittently populated with imaginary scenes of the business meetings to come or of the plane's engines failing. Are these feelings and representations the person's self state? A Freudian view considers them only partial derivatives of an inner psychic reality, of the continuously moving experience of the self.

When I think of a friend, I evoke a complex inner constellation always sponsored by the name of the friend but with discrete representations emerging upon each rethinking. Such inner constellations are subject to change, and discrete representations are liable to emerge which are determined by the vicissitudes of life, in which affection, admiration, and gratitude mingle with less pleasing feelings of competitiveness, envy, or narcissistic injury. Still, the circumstances of life affecting these representational derivatives of the internal object, in this case my friend, do not eradicate it. No internal object can be changed by eradication, although it may be altered.

The theory of internal objects does not describe or define a self state, for any episode of self experience is dynamic and complex, a matrix beyond representation. In the Lacanian lexicon, it could be assigned to the real, to that reality which is beyond either imaginary or symbolic grasp, even though *it* is there. Imagine what happens when asked to think of your mother. Perhaps you are requested to describe her. Whatever course of narrative action you take and no matter how long you talk or write about her, you never reach a point at which you feel you have conveyed that inner presence which you carry within you and which is evoked by her name.

Each of us has such relations to the inner complex. We experience *it*, we will think about *it*, and we will even narrate *it*. This is a curious position to occupy. For the part of us that stores and organizes psychic events is obviously unconscious, while the conscious part of us that experiences it aims to *think* it. But isn't to experience this internal event to think it? How can a mental phenomenon evoked within one's mind at the sound of the signifier not be thinking? Perhaps I hedge. If the psychic texture has been formed over many years by countless experiences, it has already been thought, a thousand times over; a great deal of thought has gone into its making. Further, some of the mental operations that go into it, such as thinking about a particular moment with one's mother, were never representationally considered but rather acquired in practice, such as when mother and child acted out a relational scheme between them, never subjecting it to thought proper.

As conscious selves, we thus have an intriguing relation to our mental contents, some of which are part of a moving or dynamic inner presence that we experience but cannot put into words except by partial derivatives. Freud certainly knew this. His descriptions of the unconscious and later of the id are references to an *it* within us that we cannot put into consciousness. Indeed, his theory of the dream work—particularly condensation—describes the overdetermined and cumulatively constituted internal object. As a person matures, these inner objects, added to continuously, become increasingly complex and evoke dense inner experience upon the calling. I think that one of the reasons "self" is an apparently indefinable yet seemingly essential word is that it names its thing: saturated with *it*, the indescribable is signified.

What happens when I say "Christopher Bollas"? Does the same kind of inner event occur as when I name a friend? Not quite. The sounding of my own name does not conjure the same kind of internal object. Do I conclude that I do not exist inside myself, that I have no self of my own?

It is interesting that we do not have such a precise inner experience of our own self as we do of an other, but surely it is because "we" or "I" is too near to experience to become its own signifier: it cannot call itself into delimited representation. Further, the object—not being equivalent to ourselves—is introjected into a place within our "internal world," dense with meaning but ultimately limited, while our selves are composed of all such introjections, as well as the intelligence of organization that forms the precise sensibility of our inner worlds.

We certainly try to bring our selves to a place of calling. We talk to our selves. I address this self as "you," often to encourage an action (i.e., "you should do the shopping"). The nature of this intrapsychic relation may tell us a good deal about incorporation of a particular feature of the mother and the father, who as parents were the first to address the self as "you." The individual eventually takes over the "you" address from the parents and in this linguistic transference inevitably inherits some of the psychic consequences.

As Robert Nozick says: "The self's special knowledge of and relationship to itself is expressed at the linguistic level in the use of such terms as 'I,' 'me,' 'my,' in contrast to proper names and definite descriptions" (71). But this "I" has no direct relation to "me"; it must go through the other first. "Will you give it to me?" "I would like you to spend time with me." What does this linguistic route between the I and the me tell us about the self?

It seems to identify one crucial path taken by idiom.

"Where have you been?"

"Who, *me?*

Why the need here to verify the self as "me"? A comic version has the person looking over his shoulder, hoping that someone else is being addressed. This comic moment expresses a fundamental structure to the signifier "me," part of the experience named by *self*. "Where have you been?" "What have you been doing?" "What have you been up to?" Such interrogations betray the inquisitiveness of consciousness in the face of the dynamic and never-ending wanderings of the unconscious self, which travels to worlds far from consciousness, encounters many a phantasm, gets up to many forms of mischief, and though always somewhere around escapes location.

"Of course you, who else would I be talking to?"

To the me. And the curious act of self effacement is ironically enough a very accurate interpolation. For the overwhelming amount of *our* time (i.e., the time of differing parts of the self) is spent in unconscious activity when we are lost in thought.

The presence of *me* also re-stages early history, for a child encounters many a thing, endures many an event, imagines many a phenomenon under the aegis of infantile amnesia and will not recall it. "So where were you?" we may ask. This is one of the questions a patient asks of himself when he enters analysis. Where was the self during its early history? Consciousness can only respond with a comedic counterquestion: "Who, me?"

If the me is situated in relation to the I only through the place of the other, it is also the part which has been, among other things, the recipient of parental care and parental projective identification. The linguistic partnership reflects the self's history. Where have you been? *With Mother. With Father. I think inside Mother. Inside Father. Between them. At their disposal.* But what have you learned? "Who, me?" The voice of the comic disavowal affirms that this wandering explorer of other worlds is without its own tongue: the me cannot speak. This is the preverbal self, always without words, silently exploring the textures of experience. There was a time when people said "me-thinks," but this archaism has been displaced by the less feudalistically affiliated and more entrepreneurial voice of the I. Yet the "me thinks" was a rather wonderfully simple voice, rather dumb, which spoke for a type of experience deep inside the self. In fact, the near muteness of "me thinks" seems its voice, seems saturated with the residues of vast unconscious experiences. How are we to reconcile the paradox that part of the core of us is an apparently absent presence rather than an articulate, active subject?

I think I know.

I believe that each of us begins life as a peculiar but unrealized idiom of being, and in a lifetime transforms that idiom into sensibility and personal reality. Our idiom is an aesthetic of being driven by an urge to articulate its theory of form by selecting and using objects so as to give them form.

Freud's theory of the id was a bold attempt to conceptualize this inner complex that fashions being. Borrowing from Groddeck, he used the German phrase *das es* (the it) to identify an impersonal force informing human logic. But the id was doomed, overwhelmed by too many significations to be used theoretically, and psychoanalysts became more interested in the ego, a clearer concept. Winnicott made a further attempt to represent the "it" through his idea of the *true self*, which he linked to Freud's theory of the instincts but which was also to stand for the "kernel" of the subject's self. This was the inherited potential that indicates its gestural presence through spontaneous actions; for Winnicott the concept of the true self became more important as a signifier of signs of life than as one signifying compliance and capitulation.

Both conceptualizations allow us to address the "it"

inside us. I suggest, however, that the word "me," which also defies direct knowing, emphasizes a slightly different internal movement. First, when we think "me" without reference to any other term, we evoke a dense inner constellation, a psychic texture, existing not in the imaginary, although it yields derivatives there, but in the real, an area that can be experienced but cannot be represented in itself. I am aware that writing about such a mental phenomenon is not only hazardous but based on the false premise that the elusive "me as real" can be written about. However, I shall do so, for I think it is part of the phenomenology of *this* object relation: the relation of consciousness to an internal object that is sensible, that can be felt, even though it has no voice.

The me can be conceptually identified and its material discussed. It is composed of memories (including the history of desire), and these constitute the cumulative psychic outcome of idiom's theories and their enacted deployment in a life's experience. Many thousand experiential episodes, in which one's essential idiom meets up with its fate in the domain of lived experience, leave a vast, intricate web of derived senses, a kind of metaphysical synthesis, something which though part of us is not determined by us, arrived at through our peculiar engagement with the chance arrival of objects in our lifetime. This *totality* is an internal object we designate through the signifier *me*. The curious truth that me is an absent object and yet is felt to be the very core of my authorized actions is part of the intrapsychic history of the me, as the it's fate or destiny, as a voiceless core of being that has no direct representation but nonetheless in-forms gestures and consciousness.

———

The psychic texture of any episode in a life history can be evoked by name or memory. If, for example, I think of an evening in Oceanside, California, when I ran 220 yards for my school's relay team, I can psychically feel the trace of that moment. It is inaccurate to say that this feeling is equivalent to my discrete memories of that evening: the buoyant warm sea air meeting up with the desert chill, my teammates' exuberance over winning the race, jumping in the air, the sheer bliss of running in the night, my new Adidas track shoes, the coach showing me my time on one of his watches. These images are only derivatives of the inner presence that is activated in me when I recollect that night.

In fact, life is such that an inner sense of a remembered moment may occur to me in the flash of an inner eye, a mere fraction of a second, as it emerges in a chain of other senses, and yet it will have been there in its entirety.

Evocative psychic states may be called into inner experiencing by a name (i.e., track and field, Oceanside, Adidas), or by chance encounters (meeting someone from Oceanside), or by deliberate self recollections (recalling the events for narrative purposes), or by the environment (feeling warm sea air meet up with a chill), and also by the effect of the other who left a trace of his or her being in our inner world: not an image of the person, but a psychic texture composed of a vast network of psychosomatic processings of the other collated into an unconscious organization that is called into feeling when we evoke the other's name.

The self is such inner presences.

We may rightly wonder if such an interesting fact affects the nature of our mental processes and capacities. For example, a young child learns arithmetic and over the years his study of arithmetic marries up with his cognitive development, enabling him in adolescence to have mathematical skills and indeed to have a part of his mind *trained* to perform such mental operations. Bion argued that the need to think thoughts forces us to develop a mind, this eventually leading to the development of mental structure. Similarly, we may say that self experience invites us to entertain its nature and appreciate in consciousness the particular feel of self states and emotional experience. Although this experience is too dense and psychosomatically intricate to be represented in itself, this is not to say it does not exist within our being, a unique area open to a special form of *inner perception.*

When we are interested in such inner objects, we develop an increased sense of them, repeatedly attending to psychic textures. This suggests the interesting conclusion that the sensing of self is open to development and increased skill. Ordinarily the phrase "sense of self" is taken to mean the sense of self that each of us has, but I shall give it a slightly different definition: the capability of perceiving the self. A separate sense. A sense that is only a potential in each person, who is born with this sense capacity, and who will, to a greater or lesser extent, develop it.

What value, if any, do we place on this capacity? That such a psychological talent is derived from repeated inner experience of self shapes, that the sense seems inextricably linked to and derived from the history of self experiences, brings the acquisition of language to mind, for speaking a language derives from the repetition of the language experience. If we have an appreciative sense of the self's experiences, isn't it likely that the organizer of such inner constellations will be unconsciously aware of introspective delight? This is no more than saying that a performer enjoys the appreciation of an audience, except that now we are saying that the ego—the intelligent psychic organizer that coordinates self experience—has its own sense of being considered. Such endopsychic partnership—a generative narcissism in which the individual's increased sensing of self is appreciated by the ego that constellates self experience into internal objects—suggests that such a director will make its productions more available for consciousness.

If the ego appreciates the individual's sense, then there is an intrasubjective sensitivity; I think that poets, painters, musicians, and others engaged in creative work feel pleasure in their ego's contribution to this separate sense. Is it an occasion for the unconscious to pirouette and perform in the dimly lit world of the preconscious, with consciousness turned now inward, as Echo to Narcissus? I think so. Creativity in unconscious work responds to any audience delegated by the self.

In a psychoanalysis, we may observe a fascinating intrapsychic rapport develop, in which the analysand's introspective receptiveness is sensed by the ego, which responds by being more open. And we know that this evolution is substantially contingent upon the analyst's creating a sense of rapport. By remaining quiet for long periods of time he conveys his interest in the weight of the analysand's words. Silence gives the patient's words psychic value, as the free associations echo in both participants' minds. On the other hand, analytical intervention is usually directed to the patient's internal world, to the self and object representations, to the polyvalence of words, to the image saturated with condensed meaning; this kind of analytical attentiveness is unconsciously understood by the ego that now performs its work with a welcome audience. In turn the analysand builds up in his or her mind an increased capacity for attending to the textures of intrapsychic life.

The developed sense supports the significance of the nuclei of self constellations as valued objects, even though these psychic textures cannot be directly known. The sense of self supports and increases the inner knowledge of psychic shapes in one's being. One comes to know of oneself, even though such knowing shall remain substantially unthinkable, albeit felt.

————

When Freud described free association as *Einfall*, he meant that in the course of talking to the analyst, an idea would suddenly fall into the patient's mind from nowhere. Winnicott's model imagines a different psychic surprise, as the individual falls into an inner experiencing entirely contingent for its effects upon cessation of speech and the loss of social awareness. It's as if the patient disappeared for a while. Winnicott may have found a niche in psychoanalysis for an experience valued in some Eastern religions, in which the "ego" cracks up, in which coherence or self narrative is regarded as a defense, and in which the path to knowing the self can be achieved only by forgetting this self . . . temporarily. Freud began this process when he said that self abandonment was intrinsic to the process of free association, and Winnicott added a vital next step with his idea of regression to dependence —from too much dependence on the mind to an object relation in which the analyst takes over mindfulness, allowing the patient to commune with the self's psychic textures.

There are moments in a psychoanalysis when patients are lost from insight, having slipped through a door into speechless inner experiencings when they are only with their selves: lost in them, experiencing them, traveling through their textures. The word "self" seems apt in such moments: it names an essential elusiveness, an organization in being that is inexplicable, that cannot be represented or located. Our patients are in a world elsewhere. When they emerge from this place, they reflect *on* it, tell us *about* it, are moved *by* it, often in conflict *with* it, always *under* its influence, but inevitably *beyond* its boundaries.

———

As each person has sequential inner experiences, which we call self experiences, does it follow that he or she has a self? Do we need to argue that such a self exists? Why can we not settle on the notion that we have successional inner experiences, but that no superordinate psychical entity exists which is either the sum of the self states or their coordinator?

We can conjure any vivid self experience simply by recollecting it, but we cannot evoke our selves by speaking our names or any other invitational act. A self experience seems ready at hand upon its calling; the self, as a presumed psychical entity, seems nowhere to be found.

Psychoanalysts are usually thrown into the problematics of the self when a patient claims to have no self. Some time ago an adolescent patient told me he did not have a self and did not know what this term meant. He said that if he asked himself what his self was, he received no reply other than a kind of horrid sense of emptiness that was truly frightening. He asked me to tell him what a self was. Could I define it? The anguish in this young man was so intense that I felt a need to come up with the answer, but all I could think of was how irritatingly elusive this word was. I could not see how he could be in such anguish over something that the word "self" designates when at the same time he could not feel this "self." The absence left both of us sensing that something horrid was afoot. I can still see the look on his face. My silence seemed to add to his fright.

Then I said that I experienced his self. I was not sure why I said this to him—it was a spontaneous comment, but the effect was immediate. He calmed down. He looked very hard at me, as if trying to discern what exactly I saw in him. I said I thought he was trying to look into the mirror to have some confirmation of how the mirror gets an image to reflect, that he wanted me to demonstrate to him what his self was. He nodded.

I said that trying to supply him with sight of his self reminded me of efforts he had made in the past to grasp the true meaning of a given word. He would repeat a word, such as "chair," until the signifier no longer called up the signified, until the sound meant nothing, and this would cause him great panic. Now he was doing the same thing not only with a more crucial signifier, self, but while looking at his body to see if somehow or other he could spot the self emanating from it or somehow triggering a spontaneous inner sense of what his self was. He agreed. Somewhat to my surprise, I said that this was a word which gave us access to the unobservable—but not the observable—presence that is us.

By the end of the hour he was no longer in a panic, and over the following sessions he was clearly less distressed over the question of the self. What had changed? What had precipitated the change? Was it my statement that I experienced his self? It rang true, although neither of us addressed what I meant by it. Was it my comment that he created panics by overintense scrutiny of the essence of a word—in this case the idea of a self—which vaporized its meaning and precipitated a crisis within? This did have significance for him; he knew from the analysis that he did this kind of thing, bringing about acute states of depersonalization.

But these comments were not what helped him recuperate from his panic. Instead, I think it was my containment of his anxiety which allowed him to come back from such deep fear. When he posed this most vexing question, he put me through the anxiety that its problematic raises, and what did I do? He saw, not that I had an answer to it, but that I could find some way to live with the section in the library of consciousness marked "unknown" which this word signifies, that I could live with my own doubts as to its meaning.

And yet it was clear that his absence of a sense of self was quite terrifying indeed. He described how his internal conversations were not with some seemingly knowable (even if illusory) thing called self but with a kind of empty space. He would preoccupy himself with daily agendas, going over what he would do in the next week, the next twelve hours, the next five hours, the next hour. He wrote lists of intended actions. He thought about them a lot. "And that is all there is to me. I don't have anything back. I just think and think about what I am going to do, where I am going to do it, and whether I can proceed to do it." He lived in a perpetual present, with no past, and a future made up only of projected present moments linked by the agenda he set.

He had little reflective capacity and seemed impatient with the whole idea of looking back on experience. Yet he never had any difficulty describing a self experience. He could portray in minute detail what he had done in the afternoon, and could tell me the feeling of the doing and recall any memories it evoked or desires that sponsored it. So he did not like to look back on experience, but he could do it.

One can describe self experiences, then, but still have no sense of what is meant by the word "self" and still claim to have no self; self does not seem to arise out of an inner summation of a person's episodic experiences. An individual can describe the sequence of inner experiences but still sustain the idea that no self exists.

Another patient came to analysis when he was in his early seventies. A highly successful art dealer, he had always been a depressed man and was now close to suicide. For years he disowned his own personal creativity, insisting that the analysis define itself only in relation to his "failures," which he invested with great mental energy. Significant headway was made when he began to understand his preference for what I metaphorically termed "negative capital," which he loved to invest in a "negative bank account," deposited against a future in which positive capital might upset this investment. After several years the metaphor was extended to include the notion of a "secret Swiss account of positive capital," that he did not want the world to see, because he would then lose his "credibility," which rested on the presentation of a negative self that used personal sourness to gain certain advantages in his business. Analysis of his unconscious omnipotence —insisting on banking the negative until only the positive was guaranteed by the gods—also helped him to understand another aspect of his investment in the negative, as did further analysis of his envy of those whom he saw as sustaining a smoothly running life. Ruining himself to spite his envious self, to spoil in advance the objectification of his own wishes, and realizing the competitive others, helped him understand his omnipotence and his negativity. But only when, after four years of analysis, we grasped a very particular feature of his contempt did he truly change.

He began one session, as he often did, by saying that he knew from what others could say to him, and indeed from a certain objective part of himself, that he was a person who had accomplished many things, but actually from his point of view anything good that had ever derived from him had really, in truth, been a matter of "good fortune" and "luck." He bemoaned that he, unlike other men who were highly organized and knew exactly why they were doing what they were doing, had to sit around and wait for good fortune to strike. He reproached me, saying that although I had helped him to understand himself, I had nonetheless not understood that he really was a man who accomplished what he did purely in ways that were incomprehensible to him and came about merely by chance. I said, "I think you have an omnipotent wish to be conscious of the unconscious when it happens, so that you can possess it, and as you cannot, you project this capacity into other men, whom you then idealize and envy and to whom you compare yourself disadvantageously."

He was quite struck by this interpretation. "Where did you get that?" he asked. "It occurred to me," I replied. "Well, that's true inspiration, because, you know, I think what you have said is more correct than anything else you have said about this. You are right; I do imagine that others have an ability to be the managers of their unconscious and I do not." I replied, "You say it is an inspired idea when it derives from me, but when inspired ideas come from you, you say that they are only moments of 'fortune.' "

We discovered that when an inspired idea occurred to

him, he would wonder: Where did that come from? And because he did not know, he repudiated himself as its originator. What seemed an act of almost sacrificial honesty revealed itself to be a pernicious expression of his omnipotence. If he could not know the origins of the ideas that came *from the self*, then he wanted no part of it. He wanted everything: he wanted to take possession of the self from which the inspired idea emerged, and if he could not know this self, then his hate of it was such that he would deny its creativity and insist that the idea was only an act of fortune. The working-through of his frustration over his inability to know the origins of inspired ideas gave him an increased appreciation for the mystery of being a self and diminished the intensity of his self hate; in a way, it also raised his appreciation of just how mysterious it is to be a conscious being in relation to the unconscious parts of one's being from which involuntary, unguided, inspired ideas arise.

What contributes to the belief in the self—which apparently is noticeable only when it ceases to exist and we panic over its loss? We speak of a sense of the self—and earlier in this chapter I suggested that this sense is a certain type of internal work that enhances our appreciation of the self—even if this does not lead to an increased knowledge of its meaning. We can develop a sense to sense the self which brings us closer to the object of that sense. But what is it?

———

What are you sensing when you sense your self? (I am excluding derivatives such as self representations, object representations, or moods; I am after that thing which gives birth to such expressions.) In a way, it is a kind of presence, isn't it? We have a sense of a presence in our being, a sense of our own being. We feel we are here. This is different from saying that we have evidence of being here: we can look in a mirror, gaze around for evidence of our being, but the sense of self is different: we have a direct feeling of an inner presence to our being.

But how is this different from saying that one has a sense of one's respiratory system, or the soma's intersystemic intelligence, or indeed an endopsychic projection of the sense itself? How does one not know that one is sensing the presence of the sense itself, projected into a vacuum? Couldn't a sense of self simply be a highly organized wish that conjures its object and then develops a wonderful intrapsychic romance?

I shall come to my reply by analogy. We all know what it feels like to be deeply immersed in a novel. Novels have their own atmospheres. The themes expressed in novels are usually relatively common, but the pleasure of being inside a special novel depends on the unique way the novelist fashions this world for us to live inside. The same is true of music. When I listen to a Mozart symphony I am clearly inside the moving atmosphere of a highly distinctive intelligence, instantly different, say, from that of Anton Bruckner. One has a belief in one's self because each of us is aware of having an internal world that is intelligently informed with its own unique atmosphere, a very peculiar aesthetic that creates within us our spirit of place.

But can we feel our own being in a manner as precise as the way we feel the atmosphere of a Jane Austen novel, comparing it to the feel of a Dostoyevsky novel? Well, in a way we can, and in other ways we cannot. Certainly we are conscious of thematic patterns to our perceptions, imaginations, verbal representations, gestural expressions, and so on. But to what can we compare this? Can we compare it to another person's sense of his self? How would we know what that other person is feeling as his spirit of place? We can't know, can we? However, even if you do not know the character of your self precisely, because you are part of it and lack the distance necessary to experience it in that way, you nonetheless know that your spirit of place does constitute your self. This allows you to abstract a notion from the feeling that sponsors a belief that launches this word "self" into the language with a very specific psychic charge behind it.

Each of us, with many internal objects, develops an acute sense of how these objects differ from one another. But as we cannot compare our self experiences with another person's, we therefore cannot develop a definition that derives from difference.

We cannot conjure the spirit of our own selves.

Nor can we gain it from the other who has had us drift through him. If we hold the other to account, saying, "Right then, you've had me, tell me what my spirit is," I suggest that the other will look at us with absolute astonishment, as such a task is of course impossible. "But you just told me," we may respond, "that my name evokes a fully identifiable feeling within yourself, so then tell me what it is!" A harried person might try to talk about what that inner object gives rise to, and to come up with an image here, a memory there, an observation of this, an abstraction of that. But can he transform the spirit into the intelligence that it is and was?

The answer to this is a disappointing no. Absolutely not.

Can one not, however, gain through introspection a feel of the very particular self one is? Does one have no object for one's sense of self to sense?

The feel of an inner logic, the movement of desire, the dissemination of interests, do yield a feeling that one is invested by an intelligence that guides one through existence. You feel its effects, and it is through introspective awareness that you feel the spirit of place even if you do not know its character.

We may see how intelligent an act of projective nomination it was to believe from inner experience that some kind of deity was looking over us. The notion of a God living within each of us is, strangely, an unconscious return of the projection: God as that organizing intelligence that informs our existence and leaves us with a sense of there being something that transcends and yet looks after us. Sometimes the self feels like a kind of transcendental presence, an authorizing agency, greater than the sum of those self experiences which we can know in life but unknowable as a thing-in-itself.

———

Isn't this the unconscious? It is and it isn't. Certainly both the conscious and the unconscious are instrumental in the creation of a sense of self; but the unconscious is perhaps even more vital, since the psychic construction of a self is achieved by unconscious mental processes. But Freud's theory did not address this specific atmosphere of place which prevails in any person's unconscious life—its aesthetic intelligence and structure. So when we speak of the self we are speaking not simply of the unconscious but of its endopsychic derivative. Unconscious work gives birth to the spirit of place within the individual, which is felt when it is there and terrifyingly missed when it seems to have departed.

It may seem that I am now arguing that the self differs fundamentally from its "parts." Certainly we can objectify aspects of the self and talk about them; dream contents organize self experience and are partly knowable; symptoms express unconscious conflicts within the self; and we reflect upon our self experiences continually and thus come to know certain manifestations of our selves. But when we refer to the parts of the self in psychoanalysis, we are usually referring to some of the contents of the self, its introjections and identifications, its psychic structures.

The self is not the sum of its parts.

It is an aesthetic intelligence.

———

So what can we make of those people who claim to have no self or to have lost the self? Certainly we could not argue that they have lost their idiom in being. We can see how they express peculiarity (i.e., human being). We could discuss their mental contents with them, and they would not generally disown authorship of a particular mental content. But it seems to me they are right in saying that they do not get back from that inner dream work a sense of its presence. People who are extremely distressed will speak of feeling lightweight, of believing that any breeze might carry them off; others may sit tightly on their chair, desperately afraid that they are on the verge of falling forever into an abyss. Confronted by such fears, we are compelled to take the individual's claims very seriously and push ourselves to answer the question: What exactly is the thing we call self?

It may be unknowable, but when one senses that it is there, it gives a person a sense of being the author of his existence. For a fearful person, it seems that intrapsychic contact with the forming part of being has been lost. But if he has mental contents and can be shown how his dream is unlike any other person's dream, why does this not bring him into contact with the unique forming intelligence in him that works upon the stuff of life? There is no easy answer, and I can give only a partial response.

Those familiar with ego psychology rightly suggest that the agency of this inner aesthetic is the ego, and that the word "ego" would do where I use "self." I accept that the actual dream working that goes into episodes of self experience is labor of the ego, but the person who claims to have no self is not claiming that he has no sense of his own ego, at least as I use this term. The ego is the agency of the mind that performs its mental operations, rather like the psychic equivalent of a brain. Even a person with no sense of self does have a sense that he is thinking, judging, and dreaming; he knows that he is present as an ego. His complaint is more specific than that: he urges us to realize that he does not have an inner relation to the intelligence behind the ego, to that which makes him feel guided, as it were, by some inner logic in being. Freud used "ego" and "self" interchangeably in his early writings, but later tended to use "ego" to identify an unconscious organizing skill; "self" was the subject's conscious sense of his own being. This separation of the terms "ego" and "self" is important. "Self" designates the peculiar aesthetic intelligence that informs the ego; it can be felt endopsychically as a kind of background intelligence.

Does each person have a different "feel" when feeling the self? Does my feeling differ from your feeling of your being? Or is the feel—whatever that is—more or less the same for each person? In other words, does the idiom of each subject cast a different feeling and texture into consciousness than that cast by the idiom of another subject? This may be an impossible question to answer, insofar as representation of the feel of the self is impossible, but perhaps we can compromise. I can imagine that each person who feels the unconscious factors of his own being, and who knows that at any moment he is perceiving the feel of his own idiom, shares a common experience, is feeling that which cannot be represented. Each person who engages in this unique intrapsychic task shares with others a common perceptual place and, furthermore, a similar perceptual sense, which is quite different from any other perceptual skill. And yet the very differences among people's idioms suggest to me that the factors going into an inner feel of self will also differ—perhaps more like differences we hear in different composers' music than like differences in words: not a music of the spheres, but a music of one's character, a song line in the aesthetic of one's being.

———

In order to arrive at what you do not know
You must go by a way which is the way of ignorance.
In order to possess what you do not possess
You must go by the way of dispossession.
                        —T. S. Eliot, "East Coker"

Some of what we come to know of our selves is no more and no less than the shape of what we do not know. As Freud established in his theory of free association, and as I suggest, idiom's dissemination through the use of the object is accomplished only by loss of consciousness, as one becomes a simple experiencing self. In order to possess a knowledge of who we are, we must be dispossessed of the search; only through this strange dispossession will we gain a closer sense of the object we seek, a sense that will yield us—at least as I read Eliot—the shape of our own ignorance, an ironic but telling knowledge.

He who fears he has lost the self and cannot find it is, interestingly, the very one who cannot engage in Eliot's ironic quest: unable to abandon himself to generative ignorance. A psychoanalyst will often work quite diligently to get a patient to abandon the militant question and simply talk about inner thoughts or feelings. With a schizophrenic patient he will make links between his seemingly unreferential hallucinations and his experience of events in his immediate world. More than once I have told psychotic patients the story of the anxious farmer who, alarmed when his corn did not grow, went into his fields each day to pluck the crop up by the stem to see what was wrong with the roots. In recounting this story I am telling the patients to stop looking so hard, give up the effort to see direct evidence of the meaning of being, and get to what one can know by simply relaxing and talking.

Freud's model of free association, which he regarded as a technique for the arrival of unconscious latent contents, sets the stage for all subsequent psychoanalytical interests in the self and, we might add, it sets the stage for self experience and an ironic but essential "knowing" of the self that we are.

Winnicott, Lacan, and Kohut recognized in their different ways the necessity of the other in the individual's knowing of that self. Lacan saw it as a moment of constituting alienation, but ironically enough, he only emphasized the inevitable part played by the other in the self's constitution. In the session with the adolescent patient with no sense of self, described above, I spontaneously told him he had a self because I experienced it, and this was momentarily calming. I meant that I had my own inner experience of him, one that was different from that of all other patients; on the basis of this idiomatic organization in myself I could say with certainty that he was the cause of it and therefore he had a self that was affecting me. Psychoanalysts will recognize the areas of transference and countertransference here, although in a slightly different context, as we are now considering the total effect of the patient on the analyst—not so much as an object representation, which brings up the analyst's implicit self representations, but rather as an idiom that sponsors all such representations. As patients use their analysts as their object, the analysts are shaped by the patients' desires and thereby gain an inner sense of their idiom. It is this kind of dynamic that permits us to write about the "spirit" of the other which lives in and through us long after its departure: when we think of them or when their name comes to mind, the inner feel of that person is evoked within.

As a patient works to understand himself, he unconsciously knows that such work owes much to an unconscious intersubjectivity, in which both he and the analyst affect and shape each other's self experience so as to convey information that cannot be communicated in the abstract, in articulate speech, or in diction texture; this is a cumulative, unconscious effect deriving from many differing orders of unconscious representation. We could say that this is work in the area of the self, usable only when one does not know one is there to labor away, and accomplished only by simple self immersion in being and relating. Patients who suffer from a serious loss of self or who feel on the verge of losing the self eventually recover from this terror because the analyst suggests an area for inter-being that is the outcome of generative loss of consciousness; intuition plays an important role in what one says, how one says it, in what one feels, how one expresses it, in what one wonders about and how one puzzles it, in what one senses in one's body knowledge and how one organizes it. The clinician involves the analysand in free associating, free feeling, free expressing, in breaking the overly rigid ego's observational function. This very process that Freud invented is itself curative of the loss of presence of self.

As analyst and patient shape one another, working from intuitional areas much of the time, the analysand whose self has been lost is working with a sensory system in the other who senses his self. The third ear listens to the latent contents concealed in the manifest text. The analyst's self works with an inner, intuitional ear that listens to an altogether different message, suggesting an altogether different route to knowing, one that does not yield discrete knowledge but perceives and allies with the shaping effect of the other's idiom in being. The analyst's perception may enable him to learn something at a deeply unconscious level about the nature of the other's forming intelligence, and just as the aesthetics of literature or music have much to do with timing, pausing, and punctuational breathing, it may well be that he, too, works technically— knowing when to make a comment, what diction texture to choose, when to remain silent, what image to pick at what moment, when to use his feelings as the basis of an interpretation, or when to scrutinize a word presentation. These decisions are aesthetic choices, and should be in tune with the analysand's self—namely, his aesthetic presence and its articulation. Such "technical decisions" involve work at the level of self to self, of the analyst's self sensing the patient's self, and over time he may convey to the analysand, through care and skill, a feel for how to work in this area and, ultimately, how to live with the organized ignorance that springs to mind when one thinks of the contents of the self. There is a feeling there of one's being, of something there, but not a something we can either touch or know; only sense, and it is the most important sensed phenomenon in our life. As the patient comes to know the analyst's inner ear, how he responds to and handles his self, he does not adopt the analyst's technique, but he gains a greater appreciation for the psychic skills; from this, important lessons about the dissemination and handling of the core self can be internalized.

———

We are capable of developing through our life experiences a sense of the self as an aesthetic movement that can be felt psychically. Each and every one of us has thousands of self experiences. I ride a bicycle, and it yields an inner experience linked to this object. I read a book on the American Federalist period, about Jefferson and Madison, and I enter a world with a particular feel to it. I listen to a recording of Mahler's Second Symphony, and I am transported. I am telephoned by a friend, and he puts me through his character. And so on and so on. These self experiences do not yield precise representations. Each is a condensation of its many constituents: somatic, bodily, mnemic, perceptual, fantastical, imaginary, symbolic, and so on. Self experience is too complex for representation in itself; though we can talk about or express an experience in many ways, that inner experience we have, that "in-stress," as Gerard Manley Hopkins called it, cannot be represented. However, we do something interesting with that "that," and it is a small lesson in the stuff of which the self exists—its material. We can feel the material of self in any and all self experiences, and it is this—for lack of a better phrase I shall term it psychic texture—that we use in our projections to serve the term "self."

Thus far, then, I maintain that one's sense of "self" is fashioned from several sources: from an inner feel of the authorizing aesthetic that gives polysemous (not unitary) shape to one's being; from an inner feel of internal objects which are the outcome of the other's effect upon one's self; from the shape of discrete episodes of self experience. These psychic "innards" are not the self but are closely enough linked to it to allow us to use such textures for projection: out of these valorizations in being one constitutes one's self. Such projections are not equivalent to the self, cannot be directly apprehended, but they are projections of like kind, sufficient to give the person an internal object that will represent the self, even though it will not be the self.

In his poem "A Primitive Like an Orb," about "the essential poem at the center of things," Wallace Stevens writes:

> We do not prove the existence of the poem.
> It is something seen and known in lesser poems
> It is the huge, high harmony that sounds
> A little and a little, suddenly,
> By means of a separate sense.

We think of the sense of our self as a separate sense independently contributing to that object of its perception, like a poet who, unconsciously gathering the material for a poem he does not even yet know about, gathers his observations into an inner area marked "poem to be written." Stevens writes of a poem that is the structure of poetry itself:

> The central poem is the poem of the whole,
> The poem of the composition of the whole,
> The composition of blue sea and of green,
> Of blue light and of green, as lesser poems,
> And the miraculous multiplex of lesser poems,
> Not merely into a whole, but a poem of
> The whole, the essential compact of the parts
> The roundness that pulls tight the final ring.

From the psychic instress created by the logic of our own being, from the feel of the internal objects we collect in our life, and from the textures of self experience, we create *a new object*: the self—a poem of the composition of the whole.

———

"In my beginning is my end," writes Eliot.

The mother who gives us birth also brings us in touch with death. The adult has an idea of nonexistence, not only, as Winnicott suggests, because he has come from nowhere to somewhere, but because as an infant he has experienced the continuous, one might even say generative, endings of consciousness, as he tries to perceive the gods that surround him. For every illumination in an infant's life there are long periods of sleep and darkness. Is this a form of preparation for the intrapsychic consequence, that now and then we think we can see the light at the end of our tunnel—that looks, doesn't it, like my self there?—and yet we are forever fated to live in recurring darkness, our livings ended for a moment.

I think there is a clue here to our understanding of certain psychotic patients who are terrified by loss of self.

In a way, they are now without a meaningful relation to death, not engaged in generative interplay between life and death, between origins and endings, between absolute dark and enlightenment.

Death has a particularly generative meaning in Western culture, signifying a mysterious, unknowable ending to our being, but one that strangely ennobles our existence. It is the question of all questions. What is it like to die? What do we experience when we die? Where do we go, if anywhere, in the moment of death?

These days in psychoanalysis we perplex ourselves with the question of self, but in a certain sense this word suits our secular profession and its patients because it is a personal way of objectifying the unknown. When we ask: What is the self? we interrogate the meaningful unknown; in the end, death is the most meaningful unknown we have in our large depository of unanswered questions. In previous centuries, the signifier occupying the place of the self was very likely the word "God," serving our need to objectify the place of the meaningful unknown; and the Protestant concept of the God who lives inside us all served as a bridge to the concept of the self, something that lives in and yet seemingly transcends us.

Analysts who see in this word a signifier for an elusive and yet essential organization to the person's being will inevitably respect the limits of psychoanalysis: the self cannot be addressed, found, or analyzed. In some ways the word "self" is an interrogative. One cannot ask a question of a question. "What is this?" "What is this 'it' to my being that has me organized into an evolving person?" One does not reply, "Yes, what is it?" as one gains only an echo in return: "What is it?" We are enthralled by this narcissistic discourse.

We have found a signifier that totally befuddles us, even

though it bears a truth to its word that we shall never know. Heidegger wrote, "The more original a thought, the richer its unthought becomes. The unthought is the highest gift that a thought can give." For psychoanalysts who value this word and what it designates, there is a particular disposition to the value of the question rather than the discrete resolve of the answer, for in the word "self" we have found the word that contains the highest degree of the unthought.

At the same time, surely, we see the pleasure the question provides. Perhaps after centuries of living out this pleasure in relation to the notion of an omnipotent being (our deity, of course), and after existentialism's morose wakefulness, in which death, death, and more death occupied this place, we at last take pleasure in asking this question that loves to be asked.

The psychoanalyst who believes that the concept of the self is of use recognizes the pleasure of the interrogative's relation to the unanswerable. Put to the test—"Who am I?"—the response is an intelligent echo through which we hear the question and from which we learn that the question is the only answer we shall ever have. This offers a different clinical perspective from those psychoanalytical writings that seem, perhaps unwittingly, to give technical answers to the discovery of the analysand's meaning. Bearing in mind that each analysand has a self, but one that cannot be grasped, analysts are aware that in the end the question of the self belies any notion of a comprehensive view of the subject, regardless of how deep their interpretative work goes. Indeed, some may plunge into the deep because the surface, which announces the narcissistic dilemma posed by the visage, which raises questions that only raise further questions, is too exacting to tolerate. Sight of the woods can lead many to plunge into the trees, forlornly hoping that in so doing they will gain a better access to the sight of the woods.

Knowing that in psychoanalyzing a person I shall gain only a very limited relation to his self paradoxically frees me to consider and analyze those representations and enactments that derive from his idiom. This is indeed the stuff of psychoanalysis, and it is here, in the expressions and articulations of the self, that the analyst comes to understand and analyze the patient's disturbed object relations and the marks of his life history. It is a strange but essential factor of the analyst's work that he keeps in mind what is beyond his knowing although not beyond the facilitations of the analytical process.

In setting up a procedure that can enable the patient to settle into the generative calm of a silence supplied by the other, the analyst provides a place and a process that sanctions the inner movement of self states; if time is allowed to move on, and then move on, and then move on, it gradually yields that inner sense to one's being that the word "self" designates. Such inner experiencing also includes the repeatedly unsuccessful efforts of the subject to interrogate his own being, as he always fails to come to a summative moment that stops any further meaning. But in the quiet spaces of an analysis, the patient survives these failures to know; he goes on being; and he is quite pleased, now and then, when he is discovered by his recovery of a fantasy, or a memory, or the organizing acuity of a demand in the transference. Thus will he know something of his self. But that inner feel to which he heads during the silences, that area that is so familiar and so essentially him, will always evade his effort to snatch it into representation.

———

If the self-in-itself, a phenomenon of the real, evades our grasp, it is nonetheless of continuing interest that we all have experience of a special kind that is like a visitation of the real. In the dream we are immersed in our own selves. Freud rightly saw the dream as a condensed event with a suggestive force disseminating in a thousand directions, leading to an infinite reading of its meaning. His admonition that we must not regard the manifest text as the meaning of the dream unfortunately led to a crucial failure to see in just what ways the dream also had an integrity of its own: after all, the subject is living his own ego organization! As such, each person is graced by the visitation of the dream, which brings him into his self, right into the structure of his being, taking him through its processional logic and character. Furthermore, each dream has its own peculiar unity. It has a beginning, a middle, and an end.

As the sleeper is in the dark until internally illuminated by the dream event, it is little wonder that this moment often brings to mind in poetry and literature the notion of birth, for it seemingly re-creates the evolution that characterizes human ontology—from the darkness to the illumination that is life. Indeed, each dream is rather like a lifetime, lived between the two essential darknesses that predetermine and terminate us. It has an integrity unto itself, and when this integrity is allowed to stand, the dream can also be seen as the only uncontested moment in which one experiences the self that one is as one lives *through* one's psychic structure.

It is time to close this chapter and I hear in the background of my mind a nagging voice: "Wait a minute! You have missed it, you have missed the entire point!" "Of what?" "Of the self." And I know that in a way I have, something that needed to wait until nearly the end.

When you think of your own being and when you look

back upon the life you have lived, it feels just natural to use this word "self" as somehow the proper word to designate the subjective place of your being, your lived experiences, your accidents and your good fortunes, your cultural places and your escapes, your others and their others, your body which is so familiar yet so different from consciousness, and so on. Simple yet unidentifiable, "self" is the word we use to designate our way of being, a formation that cannot be put into words yet demands a sign for itself, and for this we cast the word "self" as sufficient: it defies meaning in its own right and yet persists as a favored word.

The word "self" would not have the depth of feel to it —in spite of its extraordinary overusage—unless it linked in the unconscious to an area of designation with direct access to the core of being and existence itself. It is this that gives the word its utter and somewhat maddening simplicity. Languages other than English may or may not have a word to embody this relation—between the inscrutable yet informative deep logic of our own being and the simple object that we can perceive and say, "Ah yes, that's me, isn't it?"—a word that designates the rendezvous between the unthought known and the simplest of thinkings, a place where we just seem to live our life.

7

The Structure

of Evil

In the preceding chapters I have studied the ways in which the unconscious contributes to a separate sense—operating according to certain processes best illustrated in Freud's concept of the dream work—which can be considered the essential of creativity in living.

Although I have suggested that mental illness is a freezing of the unconscious (enabling us, paradoxically enough, to study it the more), I have deferred the question of what kind of inner sense an ill person has, or a person whose illness overpowers the cycle of condensation and dissemination that marks healthy unconscious living? Would it be a different inner sense, and if so what would this be like?

As we shall see, the person whose life is taken over by an illness, as it were, has a sense of living within something that determines him, and he may have an uncanny sense of the nature of that something which is his fate. Psychoanalysts write of pathologic structures, and we could say that the ill person has a sense of living within the logic of a pathology which, although beyond consciousness, is deeply familiar. Thus he has a separate sense, unconsciously determined and deriving not from the creative work of the unconscious but from the repetition of a pathology.

I shall consider the pathologic development of a separate sense by turning to a study of evil and of a person who lives inside an unconscious structure that both gives him a sense of his own evil and alarms us, who rightfully fear this pathology. A person who has a sense of his own evil derives it from a pathology which has unconsciously determined him, and from which he develops a logic and turns it into an extreme statement.

Indeed, the history of Western culture shows a clear and continuous effort to think about a process to which the word "evil" is assigned, an effort obscured by the evocative power of the designation of any and all horrid events or malicious people as evil. As we shall see, there is a clear structure to evil, not only a series of stages in its deployment but a psychic logic that raises profound anxieties no doubt hindering the task of *thinking* about it. Each of the manifold representations of evil in Western literature expresses only a part of the process, leaving us only partly aware of what we are trying to objectify; we remain content to use the signifier in a sloppy and indiscriminate way, allowing moral fervor to cloud our understanding.

A theory of evil nestles close to the heart of the Judeo-Christian theory of human origins. The serpent tempts Eve to eat from the only tree in the Garden of Eden which has been expressly forbidden to her: a gifted deceiver, he lures her to a fateful judgment. In *Paradise Lost*, Milton's serpent stalks Eve "In Bow'r and Field . . . By Fountain or by shady Rivulet," waiting "when to his wish, / Beyond his hope, *Eve* separate he spies." The exemplar of innocence, Milton's Eve marries angelic heavenly form and femininity, and when the serpent finds her alone at last he is struck dumb by her goodness:

> Her graceful Innocence, her every Air
> Of gesture or least action overaw'd
> His Malice, and with rapine sweet bereav'd
> His fierceness of the fierce intent it brought:
> That space the Evil one abstracted stood
> From his own evil, and for the time remain'd
> Stupidly good, of enmity disarm'd.
>
> (Book IX)

Recollecting his hates, the serpent recovers and resumes his position as the "Enemy of Mankind." Sexy, eloquent, a "guileful Tempter," it casts a kind of spell upon Eve, who, throwing caution to the wind, succumbs to her hunger. The story of the serpent and Eve is a tale of seduction and temptation, in which the "Evil one" presents himself as good and earns the other's trust. Empty-mindedness is present both when the serpent is momentarily struck dumb by Eve's goodness and when Eve succumbs to the charm of the seducer and the power of her own greed.

The link between the power of a tempter and the weakness of the subject's resolve was a familiar theme in medieval psychocosmology, and the Devil was expected to appear in disguise as an initially good figure. Kramer and Sprenger, authors of *Malleus Maleficarum*, warn the flock that the Devil tempts those suffering from "weariness," "young girls . . . given to bodily lusts and pleasures," and abandoned women who suffer from "sadness and poverty."

One had to be constantly on the alert for the Devil, who popped up whenever there was a human need, rather like an ill-intentioned precursor of social services. No doubt this belief rationalized Western culture's wariness of succumbing to first impressions that might be ill-conceived, but the power of the charmer was seen as proportionate to the recipient's need. Being tempted by an offer (of succor, wealth, or sexual gratification) involved a person in a struggle not just with the Devil but with those parts of his personality elicited by temptation: evil triumphed when the victim failed to battle successfully with the self.

The deceiver's representing the self as good to an other whose frame of mind was less than discerning, artfully burlesquing virtue, was an important part of the movement of the evil gesture. The "revenge tragedy" of the sixteenth and seventeenth centuries featured an evil plotter who befriends an unfortunate person, gains power over him, and utilizes the other's helplessness to his own end. Shakespeare skillfully represents this satire in *Othello*, as he shows how Iago appears to be good to Othello, using friendship to an evil end. Iago's success in seducing Othello illustrates how a powerful emotion, in this case jealousy, can destroy the mind, creating a murderous emptiness that has Othello throttling his love object. Iago gains Othello's trust by plying the Moor with doubts about his wife, creating a new kind of dependency, and Othello, entrapped in the structure of a spiraling psychic destiny, is preyed upon by Iago's uncanny deployment of the handkerchief, which was Othello's mother's gift to him before her death and which he has given to Desdemona. It bears in a corner a woven strawberry, the sign of nurture, and Iago's attack on the function and place of this object drives the Moor to murderous madness.

To return to *Paradise Lost*: Milton contemplates the

structure of evil in the figure of Satan, emphasizing the unconscious grief that saturates him, having experienced not simply a loss of a paradisal place but a catastrophic annihilation of his position. Ruptured from the folds of nurturance, the Satanic subject bears a deep wound and good is presented now as an enviously delivered offering. In no other Western text is Satan characterized in such effectively sympathetic terms: illuminating how loss of love and catastrophic displacement can foster an envious hatred of life mutating into an identification with the anti-life, Milton reaches the nature and effect of trauma. The prince of darkness is a traumatized soul who feels condemned to work his trauma upon the human race, trying to bring others to an equivalent fall. It is impossible to exclude from our considerations of Milton's Satan the overwhelming power and structural malevolence of God's authority, which seems grotesquely harmonized with the lust for power to which Satan succumbs.

One could point to many moments in Western literary history when writers explored the structure of evil: from the obstructive work of the Devil in the New Testament to his dank and cold presence in the atmosphere of place in Dante's *Divine Comedy*, from Defoe's *The Political History of the Devil* to Goethe's *Faust*, from the evil structures of seduction in the sentimental novels of Richardson to Hawthorne's *The Scarlet Letter*, from the complex novels of Dostoyevsky to Bram Stoker's portrait of "spiritual pathology" in *Dracula*, and from Kafka's novels to Golding's *Lord of the Flies*. I cite these examples to indicate how a civilization such as ours thinks about a complicated feature of human life over a very long time.

Psychoanalysis brings us a step further down this road, and I should like to examine this structure of evil from a psychoanalytical perspective, borrowing a new figure in the Satanic lineage to help me in my considerations. To understand the ordinary side of evil, we should look at pathology, and, as Freud did at the end of the nineteenth century, this means looking at extreme disturbances in order to understand more ordinary aspects of the human mind. It may well be that the sight of the hysteric's limpid collapse was an icon of the late nineteenth century—an individual exemplifying how repressed conflicts afflict the body—a scene played out subsequently in the collective bodies of those dying in the trenches of the Great War. One hundred years later the image of a serial killer's violent sculptures haunts the late-twentieth-century mind, objectifying a disturbing presence of thoughtless—empty, moving—violence. In the intervening century, the world witnessed two wars that annihilated all presumptions held about mankind, leaving fin de siècle man a kind of serial self, wandering through a life of increasing anonymity, the target of his thinkings, his despairings, or, in the extreme, his murders.

———

Genocide is the quintessential crime of the twentieth century, and genocide is exemplified by the serial killer, a genocidal being who swiftly dispatches his victims and converts the human into the inhuman, creating meaningless deaths that sully the concepts of living and dying. Even though these killers may be but dimly aware of their participation in an unconscious structure, and bearing in mind that the precise causes that launch each of them into his perverse existence will always be unique to the person and his lived experiences, there is much to be learned about the unconscious object relation being enacted. In the contemporary mind the serial killer is the statement of evil, and by studying what we imagine he does, we may come to understand what has always been part of our culture, our society, and the varying fates of some of our selves.

Bundy put his arm in a plaster cast now and then, presenting himself as a person in some need, reversing the usual pattern of a seducer offering his victim help of some sort. Lucas stopped his car to pick up a young hitchhiker. Dahmer promised money, a good drink, and company, in return for the right to photograph his guest. Nilsen offered a place to stay for the night. But in each case the aim of the seduction was to kill. As Nilsen wrote:

> There is honour in killing the enemy,
> There is glory in a fighting, bloody end.
> But violent extirpation
> On a sacred trust,
> To squeeze the very life from a friend? (145)

This "sacred trust" of which Nilsen writes is a trust at the very foundation of human relations, the belief invested in anyone who offers sanctuary, assistance, or nurture. Erikson called it "basic trust," so elemental that it precedes reflective consideration, almost a thoughtless assumption, derived from parental care of a child. We know, don't we, that this is the infant's and child's trust in the mother and father who look after the child, who certainly withhold any violent or murderous response, and who bear the child's greed, omnipotence, empty-headedness, and jealousies. Offering assistance to the other in need, the serial killer trades on the basic trust that derives from the child's relation to the providing world. But as we shall see, this offering that turns into the fist of death reaches the very heart of human vulnerability, and casts a sickly anxiety that spreads across society.

———

Before he began to murder, Nilsen would lie naked before a mirror and look at his body for hours on end. "As my mirror fantasy developed I would whiten my face, have blue lips and staring eyes in the mirror and I would enact these things alone using my own corpse (myself) as the object of my attention" (132). After he killed his victims, he would bathe them, put them in his bed, talk to them, dress them up, bury them under the floorboards, resurrect them, bathe them again, then dismember them, boil them, bury them, and so on. Occasionally he would sodomize the corpse, fascinated by its physicality but also "fascinated by the mystery of death. I whispered to him because I believed he was still really in there" (125), he wrote about one victim.

In his biography of Nilsen, Brian Masters traces this horrifying fascination with corpses to the death of Nilsen's grandfather: "He took the real me with him under the ground and I now rest with him out there under the salt spray and the wind in Inverallochy Cemetery. Nature makes no provision for emotional death" (47). From that day on Nilsen regarded himself as a dead man, a view that he was able to bring into consciousness according to his diaries, although obviously he lived much of his life as if this were not so.

Readers of the literature will note that many of the men who become serial killers of anonymous people have suffered the kind of emotional death that Nilsen describes. What happens when a child experiences the death of the self? Indeed, what is this sort of death?

It would seem to be the outcome of a trauma of some

kind. For example, an apparently manic-depressive patient felt at the start of his analysis that the death of his mother when he was nineteen months old was of no significance to him. However, his sense of helplessness, his lack of belief in life, his incessant yet ineffective imperatives pointed to a devastation in his early childhood. And even though his father never discussed this event and, furthermore, chided him for his various collapsings throughout his life, his father loved him, looked after him, and he was able to get on—although only just. There is no question that with the death of his mother, something within him had died, although he had been partly brought back to life by love and paternal care. He did not have that generative capacity which allows an individual to soothe the self; instead, he dealt with his unconscious grief by using his mind as an object that, through an endless supply of harsh imperatives and injunctions, was meant to boot-camp him into activity: "Come on! Stop feeling sorry for yourself and get to work!"

Henry Lee Lucas, however, was repeatedly beaten by his mother throughout his childhood. She was a prostitute and copulated with many men in front of the children. His father was a double amputee and lived, if that's the word for it, on a slat of wood, rolling himself around the village. At an early age, an angry Lucas killed animals, cut up their bodies, and played with their blood. Before going on his killing spree, he murdered his mother. I think it is fair to postulate that he experienced the recurrent killing of the self throughout his childhood as the destruction of his own personally determined self state; it had been canceled by an irreducible act that annihilated the otherwise prescient authority of his inner life. It is a *killing*, not merely death, of the self because the latter, however tragic, suggests a meaningful termination, and even though Nilsen believed his grandfather's death was the beginning of his demise, it is more likely that this identifiable loss was memorable *because* it was meaningful; it is more difficult to gather into memory the registration of meaningless killing.

The serial killer—a *killed* self—seems to go on "living" by transforming other selves into similarly killed ones, establishing a companionship of the dead, as Masters concluded in his biography of Nilsen. In place of a once-live self, a new being emerges, identified with the killing of what is good, the destruction of trust, love, and reparation.

It may be fruitless to differentiate among types of hate, but I should like to focus on this passionless act of killing rather than the passionate act of murder driven by rage. The evil person horrifies his victim and those who study him precisely because he lacks a logical emotional link to and is removed from his victim, even if transformed in fury. Stuart Hampshire has said that the Nazi killers worked in what he called a "moral vacuum"; the genocidal person identifies not with the passionate act of murder, but with the moral vacuum in which killing occurs, a meaningless, horrifyingly wasteful act. Carrying within himself this sense of horrifying waste, the killer finds a victim who will die his death, someone who will receive senseless blows.

––––

Many acts of "ordinary" murder are unannounced. A schizoid individual can kill without any prior aggressive states that might at least theoretically warn a victim of imminent danger. But the serial killer has become an especially powerful emblem of harm that may strike unexpectedly, with no warning. Popular literature and journalism portray him as quite the opposite of alarming: a friendly, if quiet, neighbor whom one might ask to water one's plants when one is away on vacation. The image of the logically trustworthy acquaintance springs to mind because of the absence of any alarming characteristics; perhaps he has *evolved* and taken on the very characteristics that allowed him to fit into the environment so that one couldn't see him!

Characteristically the victim does not know the serial killer. In psychoanalytic terms the killer would seem to be part of the environment of trust, providing no sign of danger to the victim, not alerting mental processes in the victim that might trigger lifesaving activity. The Yorkshire Ripper arises from the foggy fabric of the real that is always beyond perception yet is the basis of our imaginative re-creation of reality. Even though we know that the world is in part dangerous, and even though we are aware of our own destructive ideas and feelings, we seem able to delude ourselves that the world and the self are basically benign. This is one reason why the serial killer so alarms us: we cannot see where he is coming from and cannot comprehend his motivations, and whatever we know about him does not help us find him before he appears out of the blue and strikes again.

There is a place called *nowhere*, a country where the killer lives and from which he strikes. We know this place. Even if it is beyond our perception, we know it exists. It is the place of the split-off unknown, where actions with unanticipated consequences originate, where sudden de-structiveness against or from the self arises, a zone of darkness that weaves in and out of selves, preserving darkness and nowhere in the midst of vibrant mental life and human relations. This is where the killer lives, finding in an actual, real habitat—a bleak apartment, an empty highway, a red-light district—the objective correlative of the nowhere land that has made him its citizen. This is a land from which one never sees movement of thought or action resulting in an action that defines the self, whether the blows come from an other who lives there or from some part of the mind now colonized by it.

The shocking harm erupting in the midst of a benign texture of the real (as opposed to our imaginary transformation of reality into something alarming) is deeply disturbing, and it preys upon a certain kind of fear we have that is so great we cannot even experience it as fear: a dread that reality will cease to support us in safety and will do us harm. Some people who were victims of a childhood trauma that occupied their subjectivity—in effect displacing the imaginary with a kind of theater of the real, capable of infinite repetitions but no creative variations—realize that even more shocking than the content of what happened to them is the trauma that the real in the first place actually did something profoundly consequential. The death of a parent is not in reality *meant* to happen, and a move that takes one from one's home and friends seems only an imaginary possibility: it is not meant to occur. A child whose parent repeatedly beats him will as an adult feel not that the physical pain of the beating was so painful, or even that it was the parent's hate that was so terrible, but that something happened which never should have happened; something displaced the true self and left in its place an irreversible identification with the act committed against the child's self.

——

When the serial killer offers help to the victim as part of his lure, he unconsciously reconstructs that potential space which the self is offered at the beginning of life; dependence, hope, and belief are elicited by this gesture. When the potential recipient of this seduction is hooked, the serial killer then usually "creates" a sudden catastrophic disillusion which is precursive to the victim's psychic and physical death, a moment of total and absolute disbelief.

Gerald had a roll of gray duct tape in his left hand which he passed to Charlene with a curt order: "Tape their mouths shut first. Then do the same with their wrists and ankles. And do it right, got it?" Just as Charlene was about to clamp tape over the short victim's mouth, the girl looked soberly into her eyes for an instant and said, "This is really real, isn't it?"

(Hoffman, 43–44)

Little has been written of the serial killer's shocking occupation of the real, that terrifying moment when the grandmother turns into a hungry wolf, when the benign texture of reality mutates into something unimaginable.

Is the deadly blow of a killer who strikes sight unseen or who strangles a guest in his sleep the movement of the traumatic that cannot be seen, that gives no warning, that was never organized by an ego into a person? Pure trauma. On the other hand, is the killer who offers assistance and then, fully visible as executioner, betrays the trust, a witness that his life was terminated by a deadly other? Does he differ from the invisible killer, whose victim does not have a human executioner? When killers transport their victims through the terms of their own childhood, ritualizing their extinction by sacrificing them to a killing trauma, are the victims stand-ins for the killer-become-malignant-transcendent?

———

Georges Bataille argues that the sacrificial killing of an animal or human being gives to the witnesses of the act a sense of transcendence over death itself. They watch while a full-bodied, living being is killed. It loses its life, but the witnesses go on living. Given that all human beings are in fact "discontinuous beings," sacrifice partly serves the unconscious need to survive one's own death.

The person who has been "killed" in his childhood is in unwilling identification with his own premature mortality, and by finding a victim whom he puts through the structure of evil, he transcends his own killing, psychically overcoming his own endless deaths by sacrificing to the malignant gods that overlooked his childhood. A strange brotherhood exists between the executioner and his sacrificial victim. In some cultures the victim's blood is consumed or witnesses cover their bodies with the corpse's blood. What had been alive only moments before still feels warm; it is as if the witnesses were privy to that vital transitional moment between life and death in which neither is entirely free of the other and life is still present. The executioner is covered with the victim's blood, and the formerly alive other seems to live on, with its warm substantial presence. Dahmer occasionally cut open the body of a victim and had intercourse with the intestines, sometimes "placing his penis literally *within* the body and ejaculating among its organs" (Masters, 125). Does the serial killer who revels in the victim's blood and body seek kinship with that unconscious intermediate space—here, between life and death—because it is vital to them, the place where they once lived but where they were turned into ghosts of their former selves? Many serial killers seem puzzled by the simplicity of killing; one moment the other is alive, the next he or she is dead. What was the last moment of life? Where did life go? When did death come? Nilsen: "I was fascinated by the mystery of death. I whispered to him because I believed he was still really in there" (125). Nilsen himself was still there after his own psychic death.

———

Adolfo Constanzo practiced black magic, depositing the ground-up remains of his victim's brain in a vessel called a *nganga*, derived from Congo culture and passed on in the West Indies. Edward Humes, a journalist who studied Constanzo, writes:

The true power of Congo magic . . . lay in a miniature, magical, universe of rot, decay, and death created inside a black cauldron—a feared and secret receptacle called the *nganga*. Inside this cauldron, the spirit of a dead man could be imprisoned and enslaved . . . the single most important ingredient is a human skull and brain, preferably freshly dead, the source of the dead spirit to be entrapped. (58–59)

To imagine this object's psychic correlate is to identify an area of the self that stores and crushes the remains of a now decomposing victim.

Some serial killers seem bizarrely intimate with the rotting bodies of their victims, and they store the remains of the dead. For the killer, the rotting and decomposing others are living on after death within the incarcerated world of the killer's false self—a world designed to be perpetuated in the greater world around it. It is unlikely that he would ever consciously know this to be true (Nilsen and Dahmer may be exceptions), as he is obviously profoundly out of touch with himself, acting out parts of himself in the horrifying partitioning that constitutes the act of murder.

We should ask whether the structure of evil in this case, as a latent container, is a kind of internal *nganga*, constructed out of the remainders of the killed selves, waiting to receive the blood of a fresh victim. The serial killer identifies with an evil self that emerges from the moral vacuum created by the murder of the true self, and he also identifies with that former true self, projectively identifying it with the victim, now rotting or decaying in some roadside byway or under a floorboard or in a pot brewing on the stove. The horror over the act—the deep shock and eventual grief—is "left" to the police, medical personnel, families, and worried parties to feel.

——

There is a necrophilic aspect to sacrifice as the witnesses watch death copulate with life. Something of this can be discerned in some serial killers' eroticism: not only do they commit a posthumous sexual act but the act of murder itself is orgasmic. This death sex has its climax in an intercourse that kills—bearing the history of a childhood in which intercourse with the environment resulted in the repeated killings of the self. The primal scene's violent dimension is hypercathected, and bad fucks good to death.

It is disturbing to see "positive" sides to the act of murder, when the killer unconsciously seeks to enter the live body of the other by cutting it up in an act of "examination," a bizarrely concrete form of empathy, coming to know the other only by cutting it into pieces to look inside it. And the taboo against cannibalism—after all, eating the victim's flesh offends anyone's sense of decency—may have much to do with its unconscious attractiveness for one who has been psychically killed, because it allows him a violent alternative to the generative intercourse he has not had. Death sex is partly an effort to merge with the living, to kill in order to be released into momentary identification with life as it exits a self. It brings to mind the idea of the soul's departing the body, which may be an unconscious objectification of those moments in which the life of a self is killed and departs the body, when one feels emptied, the body a container holding only the memory of a life now putrefying. Death sex, orgasm in the act of murder, curiously transforms that moment of horror when the child's self is so shocked that it vacates the body forever, an eros stamped by the excitement of extinction. The sexually driven killer, compelled to find a new victim, may at the moment of the murder be on the verge of a horrifying panic, when the killing of his self feels close at hand; with his victim he seeks an object into whom he can project the experience (by reversal) and who will also serve as the object of a transformation of the aim, from anxiety to excitement, and finally through murder to denudation of excitation.

Dr. George Palermo, who interviewed Jeffrey Dahmer, said in court, "He killed those men because he wanted to kill the source of his homosexual attraction." The terrible pain occasioned by instinctual life can create objects of desire, and places the self in such a relation to the world that not only is disappointment a possibility but one's instincts—sponsoring urges and gestures as they do—bring one into direct harm with significant others. In this case, the instinct can feel like an endangering force. The killer's eroticism is a strange condensation of the instinct and the killing of the instinct; the urge to fuck is negated by the killing of the fuck, which results in a fuck that is also a kill. Some serial killers have reported the urge to kill like some horrid force that takes them over, but we may wonder if this isn't testimony to their vain effort to separate themselves from instinctual life itself, which is now mixed with its own anticathexes, forming a matrix of instinctuality and its killing, a pathologic combination of the life and death instincts. Confusing the object of desire with the source of the instinct, the killer destroys the object in order to be returned to a state of nonexcitation.

———

The victim's innocence is certainly part of the economics of this primal scene, and it would be ludicrous to suggest that a serial killer's victim is somehow a willing partner in the act's intentionality. But it is nonetheless true that serial killers usually prey upon the victim's need, and that need may be so considerable that it renders the victim rather empty-headed. When Henry Lucas picked up his victims along the main highways of America, each person who accepted a lift from him pushed aside the knowledge that they were putting themselves at risk. And he could certainly be charming. Disarming. And they got in his car. No doubt many were poor and could not afford the bus fare, or their own cars had broken down; they were tired and chanced it. But it is certainly part of the serial killer's intersubjectivity to put on the charm, turning an otherwise intelligent human being into an "airhead."

I would like to suggest that the "empty-headed other" is an important part of the structure of evil, for the killer finds this erotically exciting. The victim's seeming gullibility, stupidity, and lack of foresight are attractive. So far as the killer is concerned he deserves what he has coming to him. And as I have argued, when the killer announces his intent to kill the victim, his speech empties the other's head, creating a vacuum from mute incomprehension. But this airhead is also a sculpted manifestation of the killer's childlike, formerly alive self, now its victim; a form of unconscious transference occurs in which the killer's child-self lives through the victim, and the force of killing renders the self mute and empty.

Inasmuch as these killings are often acts of identification in which the victim is placed where the killer once lived, its erotic component becomes an onanistic sexuality; the killer gets off on his own annihilation. Psychic death becomes exciting. After describing in great detail how he made himself look like a corpse in front of his mirror, Nilsen concludes: "I must be in love with my own dead body" (106). The pathologic narcissism is clear: the killer is never with an other; all others being merely walking innocents, corpses of his former self, long before the Fall.

———

It is interesting and pertinent that we refer to one adult's abduction of another as a "*kid*napping." When an adult is whisked away, perhaps to be killed, there is recognition of the effect of the act, which is to subject the victim to a radical and catastrophic infantilization. Very often the victim is bound and thus made immobile. Perhaps he or she literally cannot walk. Victims are often blindfolded, so do not even have an infant's visual capacity. They may be ordered not to speak, will often have to urinate or shit on themselves, and be fed by hand. "No speak—no move" (36), ordered Terry Waite's captors. A young woman recently kidnapped in England said upon her release, "It was like learning to walk all over again," and we know that hostages and kidnap victims need time to reacquire certain adult identifications.

Brian Keenan has described his radical infantilization when he was incarcerated in Lebanon, held hostage for nearly five years. After days and weeks of isolation he would drift off into dream and daydream, the distinction between dream and reality blurred. Bodily functions resumed a profound organizing centrality. "I am reduced to sleeping in the smell of my own filth. Excrement, sweat, the perspiration of a body and a mind passing through waves of desperation. All of everything is in this room. I am breaking out of myself, urges, ideas, emotions in a turmoil are wrenched up and out from me." He daydreamed a pleasant landscape: "I feel the soft pleasure of it, as a child must feel when its mother or father gently cradles it and rubs its tummy" (67). The mind soothed him, and in such states, he wrote, "I am in a cocoon which enfolds me like a mother cradling a child" (68). Sleep became a kind of mother. "Sleep, dream, escape into the arms of those whom you love. Let them shelter you, hold you, comfort you. Sleep—the great mother" (Waite, 36).

The hostage is violently reduced to the infantile, forced into an encapsulated state in order to survive an impossible reality. Surely the killer who puts his victim through a similar collapse of the adult into the damaged child—a form of condensed infanticide, matricide, and patricide, in which all kill each other—expresses unconscious rage toward his own infantile experience? The victim is now to experience a seemingly endless, terrorizing infancy, re-creating this child's sense of *malignant* time, when mental pain and suffering decomposed the sense of time-as-development, putting in its place a no-exit time, the temporality of life in hell. Here, contained in the victim's experience, in what psychoanalysts term the countertransference, is something of that infantile hell the subject had borne, which he now transfers into the other's self experience.

———

Alongside the collective fear of the serial killer in our day and age is another anxiety, sometimes bordering on a

kind of mass panic: people wonder just how many children
are the victims of parental sexual or aggressive abuse.
That such abuse is not uncommon only fuels the alarm,
and because it is impossible to determine just how common
it is, the doors seem to be opening to a new kind of horror.

The structure of evil exploits our primitive belief in the
goodness of the other. However much a child's projective
processes may invest the parent with nasty qualities, he
ultimately knows the difference between his imagined
constitution of the parent as a monster (e.g., in dreams,
daydreams, willfully vindictive sulking) and the moment
when a parent does something that is *truly* monstrous.
When the entrusted good object suddenly changes its
nature and betrays its investment, the child is stupefied,
and his own ordinary vulnerability turns against itself.
Malignantly dependent upon the violating parent, and
often with no one to turn to, the child's dependence may
deepen; even if the abused child seems manifestly distant
from the violating parent, he feels secretly bonded to the
parent, brought closer to the very object which has be-
trayed him.

Generative innocence is essential to the life of every
developing person. It is important that one carry within
oneself a belief in "a golden era," a time when all was
well; this idealization of the past often takes the form of
retrospectively bequeathing upon childhood a simplicity
and goodness that do not hold up on closer scrutiny. But
this innocence forms the basis for an illusion of absolute
safety that is essential to life, even if we know it is a
psychically artistic device. For this generative innocence
creates a continuously renewed "blank screen" upon which
one can project one's *desire*. The child, for example, needs
to split off the bad parts of his or her own personality in

order to disseminate desire without premature closure brought on by persecutory anxieties or guilt. Even if the mother or father has been a "monster of the moment," both child's and parent's reparation needs to reconstitute a new parent, acquitted of previous charges. The innocent walk free.

The child who has been abused cannot create that generative innocence which allows the self to have blank screens upon which desire can be continuously projected and reprojected. Nor indeed can the child use that screen to visualize projective identifications of the monstrous parts of his own personality (more often than not conveniently sited in the parents). For the abusive parent has muddied the screen and it will never be blank again. There can be no intimate relation to an actual other or to the internal objects of everyday projective life that are not tarnished by the hand of the real, which has invaded the imaginary and scarred it.

The violated child has lost his or her generative innocence forever. It is a profound tragedy. People who participate in the contemporary festival of victimology trivialize the tragic effect of abuse when they insist on the absolute and irretrievable evidence of human innocence rather than the generative innocence of origins; they cannot bear to own responsibility for their own destructiveness, and can only project it into the mother or the father, unconsciously and hysterically trading on a truth. Malignant innocents, who may insist upon absolute innocence of the self throughout life and who designate certain objects (mothers, fathers, "men," homosexuals, or whatever) as perpetual villains, trade off the sympathy and need that all of us have to believe in the necessity of innocence.

It is a commonplace question to ask why a woman who is battered by her partner should continuously return to be victimized yet again. There are doubtless many different reasons why people do return to such a scene: some from unconscious guilt, others to engage in a scene of masochistic pleasure, some who have become parasitically dependent on the partner, others who have children and extended family connections with the violent man and who cannot make the break that is necessary to their long-term survival. And of course, many are simply terrified that if they really try to make a final break they will be pursued to an even more violent conclusion. Refuge from this dilemma is the privilege of upper-middle-class or upper-class women; few others can afford to disappear successfully from the homes they share with violent men, unless they have the institutional protection of a women's refuge.

Marjorie entered analysis with a storehouse of symptoms, many of which suggested her dread of a loss of self-control that might put her in an endangered situation vis-à-vis the parenting environment: she did not travel by Underground because she feared she would faint on the train; she did not go into a butcher shop because she feared that if she saw the sight of blood she would fall down and crack her head and no one would be quick enough to catch her. She was living with a gifted and colorful man who had had an exceedingly deprived childhood. He was given to occasional and horrific fits of violence during which he would beat Marjorie: she often came to sessions with a bruised face and once with a broken joint.

In part her analysis had made her partner intensely jealous, and Marjorie, for reasons of her own, had stirred him up, inviting him to imagine me as an ideal man and certainly drawing his attention to his inadequacy. Yet under no circumstances would she leave him. Her attraction to him, therefore, became an object within the analysis: initially to his phallic prowess (which was partly true), then to his ability to be atrocious and get away with behavior she would have enjoyed doing but daren't, but finally to something more insidious. There were times when she really did try to separate from him, most often after he had beaten her. Then he would apologize in a grief-stricken rather than abject way, telling her he loved her, vowing that he would never hit her again. He would remind her of their past together and tell her of what a promising future they could have, forging a potential space from the debris of the previous days. In time, she would melt. She loved him. They stayed together. She lived inside a newfound trust. Then one day, after drinking too much, he lost his temper and, in a shocking change of behavior, pummeled her especially hard. Battered, weakened, disoriented, Marjorie came to analysis having gone through a process that was now increasingly familiar to both of us.

At this point we had successfully analyzed her symptomatic expressions. Her fear of fainting expressed a wish to be held and cuddled by people, though her experience was that this did not happen. This was partly based on her mother's strident insistence on self-determinism and the rivalry she had with her mother, whom she would try to outdo by being even more self reliant than her mother insisted she be. But her experience of me in the transference liberated a different set of feelings and self and object representations, and we eventually got to the underlying wishes.

Fortunately Marjorie could see that her participation in

her partner's batterings enacted her infantile wish to be in the wonderful care of the other. Her vulnerability to his re-seduction of her expressed both her wish to be reconnected with infantile pleasures—after a terroristic rupture—and her memory of her mother's ongoing availability to her in certain sorts of ways. She could increasingly objectify the process she was inside, and in turn report it to her husband, who, though partly infuriated by this insight, nonetheless acknowledged that it now meant something. He accepted psychotherapy after a long struggle and eventually they were able to live in a violence-free, albeit turbulent, relationship.

What does this have to do with the structure of evil? It will be remembered that I am stressing the *process* of evil —involving seduction, the promise of a false potential space, the development of a stupefying dependence that empties the mind, and feelings of shock, betrayal, and the like. The victim of battering may be involved in an unconscious object relation, constituting her memory of her earliest object relations, in which she tries to accept the curative sides of the man's seductions in order to live for a while in a nurturing universe. The sequence of events, I suggest, tells us not about a sadomasochistic contract but about a need that is destroyed by the object of a sacred trust.

And the batterer? Like the serial killer, although obviously less so, he lives through his own experience of having been battered as a child, when the charm of the mother's or father's false self was used by the parent to help the child recuperate from recurrent abuse. In this respect, his evil seduction can sometimes be an unconscious act of disavowal. Marjorie's partner constructed a false self, a charming and devious self, to deal with the destructive potential of his mother and other relatives he lived with. As he charmed Marjorie back into a system created by false reparations (his mother's) with which he identifies (becoming a false charmer, aiming at all costs to avoid his wife's fury), he fashioned a shallow world of meaningless alliances that gutted the self of its passions. In the act of "unmasking" himself—when he thundered about the house throwing objects, and battering Marjorie—one can see his effort to break through the false self, which obviously released true-self states in a primitive and inexperienced form.

Marjorie and her partner both benefited from psychoanalytic treatment, and his batterings stopped. But other women return to the object who traumatizes them because in so doing they revisit the terms of their own relational origin. Something from nowhere, something purely out of sight, something without warning emerges with a violent rupture from the otherwise comforting presence of the mother or the father. The parent hits the small child violently, but when the parental storm is concluded the child and the parent return to a family situation that betrays no memory of the event. Indeed it is *as if* it had not taken place. Women who return to battering men, then, sometimes do so because of its *uncanny* re-creation of *that* violent abruption which emerges in a seemingly safe—that is, good—relation.

————

The psychoanalytic recognition that perverse sadomasochistic relations are a means of transforming the potentially traumatic effects of instinctual life, emotional experience, and interpersonal intimacies into mastered events where no catastrophe occurs is well known, and there is a vast literature on the topic. I shall not review that literature, but we should not exclude this clinical phenomenon from the present topic.

For it is patently obvious that a perverse sadomasochistic couple also enacts the structure of evil. In many such rituals, there is an orchestrated "innocent moment." Jacob, a patient in his mid-twenties, told me that he would invite a woman to his flat when he had the rather uncanny sense that she *might* be "into" what he was "into." He was never really quite sure, so he always began the evening's adventure as a very gentle and considerate host. He loved to cook and usually prepared a nice meal. He was a comedic sort of man and enjoyed being amusing, and telling the occasional joke, which brought forth "girlish" or "feminine" squeals of delight from the lady diner.

I don't think his guests actually got drunk, but they feigned a sort of intoxication, and established an ambience of vulnerability, which Jacob found exciting. At a certain point in the evening, usually after dinner, while sitting on the couch or looking at a book together, he would say quite abruptly and without any preparation, "I would like to tie you up. Do you mind?" This direct approach never failed to be shocking. The guest would be startled and, head thrown back, look at him, usually very closely.

He rarely told me of the misalliances. I am sure they occurred, and can only assume that some women readily rebuffed him, ending the evening on very clear terms. He *never* touched his female guest at any point prior to his announcement, nor did he ever try to force himself physically on her. As Smirnoff has written of masochistic activity, Jacob just "announced the contractual possibilities." It surprised me for some time just how many women agreed. Indeed, after the initial shock, they would have little or no hesitation about proceeding immediately to the act. Jacob would take the woman to his bedroom and "instruct" her. As is common in such partnerships, his personality would change from that of a humorous and animated host to a seemingly menacing presence, the threat contained by the apparent expertise of his instructional knowledge. "Here is what you are to do. You are to bend over the bed with your back to me. Good. Now turn around. Fine. Now sit down and take off your clothes: shoes first. Fine. Now underclothing." And the ritual of the undressing would occur according to his dictates; he in turn would undress, go to his chest of drawers and get his leather straps, which he used to bind his guest to the bed, lying on her back.

When the woman was in this position he would say, "Now you are completely in my power," and he would ask, "Aren't you worried?" Whereupon the guest would usually, I gather, say either "No, I trust you" or "Well, what are you going to do? It depends." So far as Jacob was concerned, once the woman indicated that she trusted him and he could now do what he wanted to her, the act was over. Sometimes he would burst into tears; other times just sit by her side—after he had untied her—and talk for several hours. He rarely proceeded to make love on that first meeting, and when he did, he never felt there was a relation between the two acts, except, of course, that tying the woman up had been very exciting to him, and had everything to do with establishing trust, which then made the sexual situation much more satisfying for him.

He was somewhat puzzled by the need for all this, although eventually he could see that he entertained unconscious fantasies about the harmful potential of intercourse, an occasion when one could be at the mercy of the other. His anxieties about the primal scene became an important feature in his treatment. He had idealized his father and seen his mother as a very castrating and frightening woman. He claimed to have lived in terror of her throughout his childhood. When she entered the room he swore that he could feel his penis shrivel up, and he described this feeling as one of his earliest memories of her effect upon him. He could never find his "proper" voice when he talked to her: it would go up an octave. Further, it was clear to him that she found his response to her presence irritating, asking him, "For God's sake, what is the matter with you?" as he perspired and some-times trembled in her presence. But he could never answer this question. He did not know the answer. His mother was a very attractive, colorful, intelligent woman, well liked by just about everyone, including his siblings, and all he could ever conclude was that there really must have been something the matter with him.

Unfortunately for this mother-child partnership there really was a series of shocking events between them when he was less than a year old. The mother had been the victim of serious trauma herself during that first year of his life; in effect, she recurrently "dropped" him and then resurrected him through guilt and great personal courage as she tried to overcome her own trauma in order to look after him. She knew, as she was to say to him years later, that her state of mind had damaged him during that first year, and I found their negotiation of a form of settlement quite moving. But try as they did to feel really relaxed in one another's presence, it was just not possible.

One of the most interesting aspects to this analysis, however, was the patient's statement that his mother would often give him "the evil eye," which sent a shudder down his spine. These early traumas had constituted a breach of the child's imaginary and illusional construction of a shared reality, and had broken the infant's peace of mind beyond his sight and imagining. This, in my view, was the basis of his reconstruction of that kind of event in the sadomasochistic acts he performed with his female guests. The terms of evil were present: the offering of the self as good; the creation of a kind of dependence and vulnerability; the sudden shock which takes the victim by surprise; a kind of infantilization. But then a recovery. The people who enact the sadomasochistic event ritualize each other's brush with a near-death experience. They enact the terms of the killing of the self, but they are survivors. However physically brusque or punitive toward one another's bodies they may be, each partner in this exchange triumphs over a much more dire event: the killing of the self.

But the sadomasochists are still trapped by their need continuously to remaster an early trauma, and although they have converted the anxiety of annihilation into the excitement of its representation, it bears the weariness of the compulsory. Jacob was fairly exhausted by his acts. Although he could not stop himself from inviting a woman to his flat, he was always filled with a kind of dread about all that *it* would require from him. This "it" which came from some other place. This "it" which compelled him to ritualize his life with women. This "it" that was so real but so inexplicable. But the act expiates the self of the secret it carries. Jacob felt that his wishes were horrific (we might say evil) but when a woman agreed to "share the experience" he felt a reprieve from a malevolent form of desire.

These sadomasochistic alliances that enact the near-death of the self, in which the child self avoids its killing but forever feels the near-hit as a kind of narrow escape, offer thrillingly close encounters with annihilation. The sadomasochist will find a companion who has endured a similar psychic event and together they bring one another to the dramatic place where such near-collisions with mortifying events are pleasurably enacted to their hearts' content. That the self did indeed once nearly meet its end, that there *was* something awful in the environment that caused such mental intensities, is an unexamined feature of the sadomasochist's life; indeed, the function of the excitement is to dull any introspective action.

We know that one of the functions of perversion is to transform an infantile trauma into a form of excitement. The trauma is represented in transformed disguise, and it is continually enacted in dramatic space with the other as accomplice, but the enactments militate against a deeper knowing of the self and its other. This is a world of makeup and artifice, of false selves celebrating the virtue of disguise and dissemblance. No one is fooled, as all know they are fooling. Innocence is represented but not believed. As Genet so brilliantly illustrates in *The Thief's Journal*, the perverse subject can live a serial life, transforming the structure of evil into a burlesque. Certain homosexual cruisers, in the best of moments "artists of the real," offer the other total care, absolute dependence, and infinite embrace—all condensed into a few seconds in a park or public toilet. Death seems to be right behind them, but always left in the wake of the swift movements and orgasmic deliveries; the cruiser's joy in cheating death is an important part of his sexual accomplishment.

———

"Evil" is a signifier that we may rightly assign to any intention or action which expresses a specific structure that, wittingly or not, is undertaken by at least two people. I have outlined the distinctive steps to the process:

Presentation of good to the other. The evil one searches for someone who is in need and presents himself as good. Even though the victim may have doubts about taking up this contract (cf. Faust), he believes that on balance he will benefit from the exchange.

Creation of a false potential space. The arrival of the apparently good one creates a potential space for the recipient. Whether because the evil one seems to possess something the recipient had always thought was forbidden, or whether because the recipient's true need now appears on the verge of being met, the subject, by presenting apparent goodness, evokes hope (or greed, or the urge for power), and the recipient views him as a potential resolution to circumstance.

Malignant dependence. When the victim takes up the offer of assistance, he becomes dependent on the provider; we may regard this form of dependence as malignant since the nurturer feeds in order to destroy, since the initiator of the structure will turn this need into a dire fate.

Shocking betrayal. Although sometimes the victim is killed while asleep or totally unaware, the perpetrator often first presents the good appearance and then suddenly and violently changes his presentation, and the victim is catastrophically shocked by this reversal of fortune—at the deepest level not simply by the individual who commits the act of harm but by the change in reality itself, which he had assumed to be relatively benign.

Radical infantilization. With the total collapse of trust and the madness expressed by a sudden dementia of the real, the victim experiences an annihilation of adult personality structures and is time-warped into a certain kind of infantile position, possibly depending now for existence itself on the whim of incarnated madness.

Psychic death. The victim experiences the murder of

being. The self that was in need, that trusted the world, that felt the arrival of a potential space, that became dependent, and that believed in a good fate, is suddenly killed.

This structure is part of the unconscious knowledge of Western man. It need not be fully deployed for the structure to be perceived; a single allusive gesture evokes its entire presence. When Saddam Hussein "entertained guests" in a widely disseminated scene that was broadcast on television, he made one fatal error that personified him as evil in the eyes of those who watched; he beckoned to a child and, resting his hand on the child's head, assumed an affectionate pose. He meant to look good. Instead, the gesture instantaneously evoked in the mind of the viewing public the structure of evil, and everyone now *knew* that here indeed was a man capable of the hideous crimes of which he had been accused.

———

Did Saddam Hussein also represent a political regime that operates within the logical structure of evil? Are governments or groups capable of deploying this structure of evil, and if so what form does it take?

Hussein's Baathist regime, like Pinochet's Chile or the Generals' Argentina, is notorious for being a police state in which ordinary citizens are subjected to a very particular kind of terror. Samir Al-Khalil's book on Hussein begins: "Salim was about to sit down to dinner when the knock came"(3)—a phrase that could relate to moments lived under a disturbing number of other regimes and that immediately captures a terror that lives in the imagination of all men and women. The individual is plucked without warning from the warmth of domestic life and taken to another place by some violent representative of the real. To account for what?

Salim was not a political opponent of Saddam, and he was incarcerated without reason. He was well treated by the police but was too disoriented to comprehend what they claimed he had done. Where had he been on a particular day some time before? He could not recall. "Dates and numbers were now being combined into single questions, and Salim was becoming so frightened he could not retain the different parts of each question, much less put them together into a coherent answer"(4); a loss of intellect obviously arising from a collapsing of the adult self. Soon he was speaking "nonsense."

The police are understandably one of the most important arms of the state and the way they behave is instrumental in the population's interpretation of its government. A benign state, one not governed by leaders who intend the people serious harm, will trade off the citizens' unconscious presumption that it wishes them well. This will happen even when police, government officials, or political leaders make mistakes, as inevitably they do, for they know that citizens understand that corruption is part of life and will forgive the structure of their state.

Terrorist states also trade off the unconscious belief in one's safety, but they do so in order to divide and rule the subjects, who may be desperate to maintain the illusion of a benign reality even when they clearly see the dangers. However appalling the serial murder is, his singularity is almost a relief: he is an isolate, one of a kind, and he can be caught and incarcerated. But what of the state that operates according to such a mentality? What do we do with the Saddam Husseins?

We try to forget about them, not simply because they pose military or terrorist threats but because it is too disturbing to contemplate their presence. We can think of military powers that concerned people but that did not evoke quite the same blanking of the mind. A Saddam Hussein is unthinkable because his regime operates a structure so evil that he undermines our most profound assumptions about human safety, a need to believe that our guardians wish us no harm.

The politics of evil trades off this need. A Baathist party will terrorize its citizens, using this need to believe in a benign parent even as (indeed especially as) it pursues its malevolent ends. Each state is a derivative of the parenting world that exists in the mind of its citizens, and a terrorist regime will exploit the unconscious relationship to obtain a denial of its terrors among the citizens, who will support the denial. The state is unconsciously attacking the earliest and most profound of human relations and assumptions: the relation to the parent.*

There are regimes which inflict appalling cruelty on their citizens but which are not evil. Only those regimes that knock on the door in the night, trading off the population's unconscious need to have a good parent, operate according to the logic of evil, and with these evil regimes that logic malignantly transcends its constituent features and becomes the voice of political terror. Caught in the structure, the population collapses. Inevitably it has to rely upon people outside the structure who, it hopes, will be able to act against the process to liberate them.

---

* To examine the psychology of torture is beyond the scope of this chapter, but the torturer illustrates a perversely brilliant exploitation of the structure of evil, as he alternates between being the good parent and being the bad parent. He oscillates from being a malevolent demon who inflicts appalling harm on his victim to being a benevolent listener who truly has his victim's best interests in mind, if only the victim would talk. This is part of the psychology of torture: the alteration in presentation of the real, designed to bring about a kind of infantile regression in the victim, who comes to need the torturer to define relational structures.

———

Political evil, which has power, is an extreme in human behavior, but all of us know of more ordinary kinds of evil. Every child will now and then be shocked by the failure of parental love. This is perfectly ordinary and common among even the most blue-ribbon parents. Mothers and fathers become irritated with their children, get angry with them, and maybe tell them to "go away." But when a parent is unexpectedly angry with the child—not in response to something the child has done—the child's shock may result in what seems like a temporary migration of his soul from his body. This is not a willed action. It feels to the child like a consequent fate, as if the parent has blown the child's soul right out of his body.

Each of us has received such an apprenticeship experience in the art of dying. We know what it is like for the soul to depart the body even though we have as yet no knowledge of actual death. We could say this is what psychoanalysts mean by the experience of "annihilation," but this experience and the anxieties attendant upon it have, in my view, been too bound to catastrophe. It is true, of course, that infants who suffer severe trauma will have an annihilation anxiety; in some cases a person's hatred of the world will be so intense he will have a talion fear of being fatally poisoned by his own venom. But each of us has a less severe dose of the experience of extinction, one which is also linked up to a concept of return. We return to our bodies. Peace reigns on heaven and on earth. We are back again. Each adult who has had "good enough parenting" will have a psychic sense of a kind of migration of the soul, sometimes shocked out of the body, but always returning.

This cycle of shocking exit, emptiness, and return gives

us our confidence, so that even when we are deeply disturbed by traumatic events—the death of a friend or a parent—we feel that somehow "it will turn out all right in the end." People can maintain this belief right up to the point of imminent death. Even knowing they are about to die they can nonetheless believe they are going to be all right.

The concept of heaven gives the Christian this kind of "turning out all right in the end" place, and other religions also provide destinations for the soul and death rites that ensure a fortunate conclusion. These are as ancient as mankind itself, for even the most primitive and ancient cultures buried the dead in special—not just dispensary —ways, putting food or offerings along with the body in the burial site, as nourishment for the journey to the other world. In the Catholic religion, a priest will be called to give the last rites to a person close to death, ensuring that the person is blessed prior to the soul's departure from the body, safeguarding it against the demons that await near the bedside. The priest hears confession and forgives the Christian for his sins.

It is this peace of mind that Othello denies to Desdemona:

OTHELLO: "Have you pray'd to-night, Desdemona?"
DESDEMONA: Ay, my lord.
OTHELLO: If you bethink yourself of any crime
  Unreconcil'd as yet to heaven and grace,
  Solicit for it straight.

When Desdemona realizes that Othello intends to kill her, she cries out, "Then heaven have mercy on me!" But as we know, she does not understand *why* she is to be killed.

Thus, although she has prayed and has called upon heaven to have mercy on her, she does not have the psychic integrity essential to the act of confession that precedes one's death. That is why she pleads for more time.

OTHELLO: Out, strumpet! Weep'st thou for him to my face?
DES: O, banish me, my lord, but kill me not!
OTHELLO: Down, strumpet!
DES: Kill me to-morrow, let me live to-night!
OTHELLO: Nay, if you strive,—
DES: But half an hour!
OTHELLO: Being done, there is no pause.
DES: But while I say one prayer!
OTHELLO: It is too late.

(Act v, scene ii)

Desdemona pleads for time, not only hoping that her husband will calm down in the morning but also so that she can compose herself before death, achieve a psychic integrity that will heal her disintegrated state of mind. When Othello says, "Being done, there is no pause," he recognizes that he has in a sense already killed her: her soul destroyed, her psychic integrity denied, her smothering is the last act of an execution that has already begun.

Few moments in dramatic literature are as horrible as this killing: Shakespeare reaches a trauma known to all who watch or read this play. The trauma is the experience of feeling deeply shocked and confused by the other's anger or rage, when for a moment one's soul leaves one's body, one loses contact with oneself, and one wonders if there will ever be a return to psychosomatic integrity again. In the evil moment, the self experiences psychic disintegration while remaining alive. Fortunately for most of us, we do return safely to our body selves after such shocks. But we know the experience, and it is to this unconscious knowledge that Shakespeare directs his evocative insight.

The serial killer has, at the very least, unconscious knowledge of a dire extinction of his own true self, but the murder he carries within him is not simply a memory of a catastrophic betrayal inscribed in his character: something has changed him, and it is this something that leads those not so destined to stand back in horror and isolate these killers as *different*.

————

When we are inclined to see the killer as the personification of evil, this transfers him to an allegorical plane as the representative of the hideous. Allegories thrive in authoritarian societies, when those in opposition try to represent forbidden ideas in personified form.

An allegorical character usually represents only one quality—virtue, sloth, seduction, faith, for example. Concentrating one quality in a single character gives a greater *force* to that quality, but it lacks the complexity of an ordinary character who might contain all these elements. And the structure of allegory, its rigidity and lack of emotional play, bears the terms of its origin.

Although allegory is an ancient narrative device, not usually regarded as a criterion of human behavior, I believe the serial killer is someone who has been allegorized: he is squeezed into an identification with one quality, evil, that obliterates other psychic qualities. As his soul departs, leaving him emptied, he identifies with the killed self, which he then distills and represents as the essence of his being. He identifies with the force of trauma and out of this fate develops a separate sense of the work of trauma, which, like Lucifer, he turns into his profession: squeezing others into his frame of reference.

Allegories involve the compartmentalization and splitting of human qualities; and an allegorical struggle involves characters reacting on each other in an externalized conflict. The serial killer sets off a chain reaction in a community and, ironically, his allegorical condition is transferred to a broader allegorical structure; community representatives are interviewed to obtain a distilled comment on this kind of evil: church leaders speak of the theological meaning of serial killing, psychologists talk about the malevolent psychosocial factors that breed him; educators discuss the failure of schools. The gruesome feature of this transference is that the killer catches the population in his pathology; everyone is allegorized and plays a part in a very precise kind of theater. Where there had been separate universes of divergent and complex unconscious evolutions of individual selves, there is now a community of the anxious, bound in the narrowing confines of danger.

Whether consciously or not, the serial killer indeed has become an individual obsessed by his compulsion to kill. The obsession obliterates the effective functioning of other parts of his personality, and he comes to identify with *the force* of his passion. The displacement of the complex checks and balances in an operant internal life by the force of an urge—this is not only the hallmark of such a person's character but the reason why the serial killer is fittingly allegorized by people, who understand that the allegory objectifies the destruction of complexity by the force of prevailing ideas.

Evil, considered as a structure, points to a complex reorganization of trauma, in which the subject recollects the loss of love and the birth of hate by putting subsequent others through the unconscious terms of a malevolent extinction of the self.

The structure of evil, then, is personally knowable to each person not only because we all have experienced shocking betrayals in an otherwise trustworthy parental environment, but also because we all have transformations to the allegorical plane when we identify with the force of a feeling—in the case of evil, the force of the emptiness sponsored in our selves by the shock *and* its unconscious marriage with the destructive sides of our personalities. All of us have experienced this trauma, and we all know its structure. Each of us will in some respects subsequently identify with it, mesh it with the mental valorizations of our own sadisms, and entertain its future in fantasy— when we are cruel to each other, or in the so-called practical joke, when we play to unfortunate (but usually not disastrous) effect on the other. (One of the most popular television programs across cultures was *Candid Camera*, a program that converted the structure of evil into comedy.) But some people come to suffer deeply by the process I have discussed, and in the extreme, these genocidal people occupy our thoughts to an unusual degree, haunting our minds as the Grim Reaper did in the Middle Ages. We fear him because he stands for execution without mercy, without meaning, without an intact soul. He is the perfect executioner for a population that has come to feel increasingly serial and meaningless.

8

Cracking Up

In *Jokes and Their Relation to the Unconscious* Freud calls the processes that construct a joke the "joke work." The mechanisms in this process are familiar to readers of *The Interpretation of Dreams*: a joke uses displacement, condensation, and substitution to arrange those acute manifest misunderstandings which convey the kind of hidden truth that always subverts. *The Psychopathology of Everyday Life* became a virtual celebration of unconscious trickery.

Freud's chapter "Bungled Actions" is a comedy of errors, a description of ordinary slips, such as dodging an oncoming pedestrian only to find that moving to the left or to the right will bring one into intimate face-to-face collision—"behind . . . a mask of clumsiness [such bungling] pursues sexual aims"; or less common mistakes, such as the one reported by Freud's colleague Stekel: "I entered a house and offered my right hand to the hostess. In a most curious way I contrived in doing so to undo the bow that held her loose morning-gown together" (176).

Freud reckoned that there would be intense resistance

to any sustained tolerance of this practical joker inside, but fortunately evidence of the unconscious as subverter of intentional speech remains abundant. We will always have a Dan Quayle, who seems to reach parapraxal genius on public stages. "Republicans," he admonished, "understand the importance of bondage between a mother and child." Or his spirited response to a television interviewer on the departure of White House Chief of Staff John Sununu: "This isn't a man who is leaving with his head between his legs." Quayle did not stop with this revelation of his sexual fantasies. He said things that allowed us to see the great potential of the unconscious to lead a nation: "We are not ready for any unforeseen event that may or may not occur," he told a reporter from the *Cleveland Plain Dealer*. Perhaps he had in mind—in unconscious mind—an earlier prophecy he had made while campaigning for George Bush: "We have been pushing the idea that George Bush is going to make matters much, much worse" (Petras, 1994, passim).

The parapraxal act places banana peels in the self's path, forever undermining the arrogance of consciousness.

Even when a self has plenty of time to work over a statement—as did Daryl F. Gates, former police chief of Los Angeles, when he wrote in his autobiography about the incident when police officers beat Rodney King—it is possible for unconscious irony to seep through a rationale: "We are the best police department in the world, but we are not perfect. Rodney King should never have been hit fifty-six times, yet many of the blows which struck him were correctly placed so as not to cause serious injury, exactly as we teach in the Academy" (Petras, 1994, 13). Perhaps the expression "the truth will out" refers as much to these violent intercessions of the unconscious in arresting the conscious self as it does to the notion of externally applied pressure to bring out the truth. Certainly Richard Nixon would concur: here is how he tried to deny White House involvement in the cover-up of the Watergate break-in: "What really hurts in matters of this sort is not the fact that they occur, because overzealous people in campaigns do things that are wrong. What really hurts is if you try to cover it up" (Petras, 1993, 33). Or consider these statements given by three separate motorists to the police, on three different days in different parts of the United States, about running over a pedestrian: "A pedestrian hit me and went under my car." "The guy was all over the road. I had to swerve a number of times before I hit him." "The pedestrian had no idea which direction to go, so I ran over him" (Jones et al., 51, 55).

The idea of the unconscious turning the self into a fool is an important part of Lacan's clinical reformulation of psychoanalysis. He ended his notoriously brief sessions with a wave of the hand when the patient's unconscious fooled him; dejected but he hoped privileged, the latter stumbled into the streets to wonder what in fact he had said to get the boot. Lacan's relish in his posture as a jester—a virtual embodiment of the unconscious as disruptive other—was well known to Parisians. One never knew quite what he would say. Nor did he. By the end of his life, for better and for worse, he had made a virtue of the ordinary folly of everyday man.

He possessed an exquisite sense of the absurd. Camus wrote, "All great deeds and all great thoughts have a ridiculous beginning. Great works are often born on a street-corner or in a restaurant's revolving door. So it is with absurdity. The absurd world more than others derives its nobility from that abject birth" (18–19). Lacan is famous for his own "revolving door," as something like twenty analysands an hour passed through it, but perhaps it is a particularly French sense of humor that makes this possible, as such violent dismissals allow for the abject births.

Too much is made these days—certainly in Protestant England—of the essential sufferings of a psychoanalysis. But pain and suffering in this confrontation—between the destructive pleasures of enactment and the enhancing loss brought by interpretation—is not the only way to characterize the structure of a psychoanalysis. Throughout, the analysand's speech undermines his authority; the mere fact of free association deconstructs any tragic hero's destiny. Indeed, a patient well into analysis knows that each session has an ironic fate: one begins with a notion of what one is going to talk about, only to discover that speaking dismantles intentions and brings up unexpected material. The self that wants to master its narration is continuously slipping up in its intentions. This aspect of psychoanalysis is an entirely different world from the tragic world where blindness meets up with insight. Here the parapraxal self speaks in an absurd space, and psychoanalysis is a comic structure; the analysand is turned upside down by the intrinsic subversions of unconsciously driven speech. A patient in analysis is straight man to his unconscious, and it is a long time, if ever, before he comes to enjoy the comedy. This is true of life in general.

Fortunately, psychoanalysis knows this and gives the patient a couch, no doubt so that he can lie down before he slips and falls.

The psychoanalyst may be said to have a sense of humor insofar as he sets this up, and each time can observe the folly of an analysand. His humor derives in part from his affiliation with unconscious processes. He can see when it makes its claim. The patient knows this, of course, and tries to cover his tracks, but the joking continues, and the analyst has subsequent opportunities to chuckle, his "um" or "ahummmmm" being the equivalent of hilarity over the amusements of unconscious action. "I know what you are thinking," retorts the patient. "You think I mean . . ." And the play continues.

A patient with a rat phobia which she had intended to remedy by behavioral techniques recalled that her fear began when she was a child lying in bed, listening to rats scurrying back and forth in the attic. A dread of what rats are up to and where they are going haunted her. Later in the session, immersed in recollecting her mother, whom she regarded as exceptionally frustrating, she exclaimed, "She was . . . erratic!" "Erratic?" I queried. "Erratic!" she replied. Silence. A long silence. An intelligent person. Pondering. "Oh, clever. Very, very clever. Well, I don't think so. Sorry, but I just don't think so"—and in a way she was correct. We didn't get to think so for quite a long time, indeed. However, she was to a considerable extent cured by her unconscious, as she became less enraged by her unconscious utterances and more amused by them. The queen of her court valued her fool, and, in time, she knew it was the fool she needed to hear.

A sense of humor grasps the absurdities of life. This is a capability that captures an acute moment, a point in the intersection of two realities: the intentional and the unintentional, conscious and unconscious. A sense of humor finds pleasure in the difference. Those who have it can see things that others without it cannot grasp. It may function even amid pain. "In the most difficult of times, in the bleakest circumstances," said the Labour Party politician Neil Kinnock the day he heard of the death of a colleague, "he never lost his sense of humour. He could always find an irony in the inconsistencies which were present."

A sense of humor also breaks down one's receptive equanimity upon encountering the ponderous. Humor would crack the intended effect of an ordinance drafted by the city commissioners of St. Augustine, Florida, who forbade nudity on public beaches. They believed they had to define buttocks, inasmuch as these were to be excluded from public view. The ordinance read:

Buttocks: The area at the rear of the human body (sometimes referred to as the glutaeus maximus) which lies between two imaginary lines running parallel to the ground when a person is standing, the first or top of such line being one-half inch below the top of the vertical cleavage of the nates (i.e., the prominence formed by the muscles running from the back of the hip to the back of the leg) and the second or bottom line being one-half inch above the lowest point of curvature of the fleshy protuberance (sometimes referred to as the gluteal fold), and between two imaginary lines, one on each side of the body (the "outside lines"), which outside lines are perpendicular to the ground and to the horizontal lines described above and which perpendicular outside lines pass through the outermost point(s) at which each nate meets the outer side of each leg. (Petras, 1993, 106)

Try to imagine, will you, an unsuspecting good and earnest citizen of St. Augustine encountering this sign as he is about to go to the beach. Unsure quite where these lines and folds are—and how visible they may be, lest he violate the law—he may feel he has no choice but to undress and ask a friend to help him find them. Scores of previously clothed St. Augustinians might well be pushed into unintentional nudity simply in order to understand this city ordinance.

The commissioners would be unlikely to find this amusing. And we can say that they lack a sense of humor. Sometimes those caught up in the solemnities of life can't be humorous—or humored—in the heat of a given moment, but only later, when they can reflect on what happened.

In the late 1960s the Student Mental Health Center of an American university shared the second floor of a drab, colorless three-story concrete building with a dental clinic. As one approached it on dreary winter days—usually overcast, wet, if not blizzardy—one's mind needed to hide from these everyday facts of life. So it was no doubt the case that the intelligence quotient of many a soul plodding up the slippery slopes on an ice-stormy day toward this dull building was dropping quotients with each step. Perhaps this is what happened to the person I am about to describe.

I received a message from my secretary, who worked in a small office walled off from the waiting room, that my new patient had arrived. As was my custom, I said I would come out to collect him. She did not see that he had left the room, since she could not see anyone in the waiting room once she sat down after responding to inquiring patients, because the opening between the two rooms was some two feet above her head. She could not have known that he had decided to go to the toilet for a quick evacuation before he began his session—which psychoanalysts term acting out. Nor did she notice the unannounced arrival of a stranger in the waiting room who took up a chair and waited impassively.

I arrived, said hello, and asked this awkward youth to come along. We walked down the hall some thirty feet to my office and then sat down, I behind a desk, he in a straight, rather uncomfortable chair. It was my habit in those days—having been inspired by classical psychoanalysts—not to say anything at the beginning of an interview but to allow time to pass. After five minutes of silence, when I only occasionally looked at the patient—casting my glance instead at the wall, at a calendar with a California beach on it, out the window at the ice drops racing to the ground—I saw that this already pale youth seemed to have lost any remaining blood in his face. I said "Yes?" and he replied, "Ummm . . ." and stammered something. A few more moments passed, and I looked at him again. I asked, "What brings you here?" He looked exceedingly worried. "I am in a lot of pain," he said; minutes later, his fear looked like panic. I said, "What kind of pain are you suffering?" He could barely mumble the words, "In my mouth." "Hard to speak about your pain?" I replied, wondering now if he were psychotic.

My line of thought took me to recent papers I had read about mad people. I had just been reading some of Harold Searles's work, and recalled his description of a patient who, when told that he could not have his cake and eat it too, replied with immediate outrage, "Cake . . . I don't want any cake!" So when the patient told me a few minutes later that he had a pain in his tooth, I thought for sure I had what Searles called a concrete patient on my hands. The phone rang, however, and interrupted my private musings. My secretary said, "Mr. Bollas, your patient is still waiting for you." "I am with the patient," I replied. "You are?" she responded, her chair shrieking across the floor. "Well . . . I see him right here . . . in the waiting room . . . Who . . . who are you with?" "Who am I with?"

I said, irritated by her incompetence. Embarrassed, I turned to the patient and said, "I am sorry, but could you tell me who you are?" This is a sinful request for a therapist to make to a patient who is clearly in the midst of an identity crisis. He gave me his name, I repeated it to the secretary, and she informed me that this was not the name of my patient but of someone else. For a brief moment—and I don't wish to overstate this—I thought to myself that this was now a very psychotic patient who had made no arrangement whatsoever to see a psychotherapist but simply walked into the waiting room under the bizarre presumption that he could enter therapy without arrangement. My confusion ended when this bashful, frightened young man asked, "Are you a dentist?"

I told him how the error had occurred and apologized, but when I said I was a psychotherapist I confirmed every suspicion he had ever held about the lunacy of our profession.

Circumstantial amusement when the self is caught up in a reality that makes less and less sense is the basis of one of television's most popular programs: in the United States it is called *Candid Camera*, in England *Beadles About*. The invariable form of the practical joke here is a prank played upon an unsuspecting person who finds that his assumption about reality is undermined by the turn of events; increasingly puzzled, he believes that surely *he* must be mistaken, and whatever might be amiss, if anything, will be corrected in time, or understanding will prevail—but no such luck. Instead, reality seems to go crazy.

If the unconscious subverts the intentional subject, so too at times does circumstance. "At the heart of all beauty," writes Camus, "lies something inhuman, and these hills, the softness of the sky, the outline of these trees at this very minute [when "strangeness creeps in" to the observer's consciousness and he perceives the "density" of the world] lose the illusory meaning with which we had clothed them, henceforth more remote than a lost paradise." He concludes, "The primitive hostility of the world rises up to face us across millennia. For a second we cease to understand it because for centuries we have understood in it solely the images and designs that we had attributed to it beforehand" (20). Whatever we know or think we know about this world, it may—and does—sometimes act in ways beyond our comprehension. This is not news to children, who are forever finding that the real does not cooperate with what they believe they know of it or with how they imagine it. A blow from unimagined or unforeseen reality is a common fate for children. And the practical joke of *Candid Camera* trades off *this*.

Inspired comedy often mixes the subjective parapraxal and the circumstantial to create a demi-dream. In "The Psychiatrist," Basil Fawlty runs to the kitchen in alarm to warn his staff that there is a psychiatrist in the dining room. He has not heard the psychiatrist discuss with his pediatrician wife how the Fawltys find time to take a holiday. But psychiatrists read minds and believe people are always thinking about sex, and when Basil returns to the table, the psychiatrist asks, "How often do you manage it?" The scene proceeds:

BASIL: *(taken aback)* Beg your pardon?
PSYCHIATRIST: How often do you and your wife manage it?
BASIL: *(stunned and speechless)*.
PSYCHIATRIST: You don't mind my asking.
BASIL: Not at all, not at all. *(nervously)* About average since you asked *(trying to recover)*.

WIFE OF PSYCHIATRIST: Average?

BASIL: Uh huh.

PSYCHIATRIST: What would *be* average?

BASIL: Well, you tell me!

WIFE OF PSYCHIATRIST: Well, ah . . . a couple of times a year?

BASIL: What?

PSYCHIATRIST: Once a year? . . . Well, we knew it must be difficult. In fact, I don't see how you can manage it at all.

BASIL: Well . . . as you've asked . . . two or three times a week!

PSYCHIATRIST: A week?!

BASIL: Yes, it's quite normal down here in Torquey, you know. *(Exiting in a huff.)*

Thus does a comedy of errors blend the impossible waywardness of the circumstantial and the subject's unconscious self. The parapraxal and the accidental seem almost made for one another. If there is no resolution to the absurd condition of man, as Camus would argue, is there possibly some form of pleasure to be found in the play of these two rogues? Is there something in what Winnicott called the third area, as the self slips between his subjectivity and world implacability, that constitutes *jouissance*? A child does not notice a toy falling in front of him; he bangs into it and almost falls down but doesn't, and anxiety turns into laughter. Desire meets circumstance. Something in the meaningless encounter—or the encounter of meaninglessness—becomes enjoyable. Experience of the error borders on anxiety, indeed is often close to true danger, but the self escapes, and in the end it is a laughing matter.

Two people who happen to sit next to one another on the subway strike up a conversation. They discover they are traveling to the same stop, indeed learn they live on the same street, finally find they are man and wife. Here in the encounter between the bizarre creations of the unconscious and the thoughtless events of the real world —between the agility of absolute determinism and the resolute dumbness of pure accident—Ionesco finds joy.

Is this the *jouissance* of the absurd?

The comic mode, then, in which the world is turned upside down and then righted, is a brief marriage of the subjective and determinate to the consequential and indeterminate, out of which a separate sense—grasping and enjoying this play of opposites—evolves to become a sense of humor.

Some time ago, a colleague said to me that an intended action on my part would take courage. That night in a dream I observed a rather large assembly of medical personnel and family discussing my plight. As I listened, I thought I might still be alive: they seemed to be talking about potential medical interventions. The dream space opened up further, and now I saw myself, or what I knew to be myself, lying on an operating table—or was it an autopsy bench, I wondered—covered in a sheet from head to toe. That worried me. I thought it was best to lift the sheet to see how I was doing, and found that I was a chicken. I never thought, Oh, there's a chicken, for this was clearly me. In fact, I was a roast chicken, rather well done. As the dream faded, I thought to myself that I looked rather well, considering.

On waking, I realized that this unflattering dream was my response to my friend's call to courage. I was "dead meat." I had "chickened out," and the dream expressed my fear that I would not be up to the task. This dream was a comic event and I was the butt of my own unconscious.

Every time we move from wakeful reality into a dream

and back out into wakeful life, we traverse a route from relatively conventional existence into the upside-down world of the comic universe. The ego that constructs the dream shares with comic intelligence the tasks of right timing and correct spacing. The chicken dream opened a new space at exactly the right time to bring me into a new and different view of myself, with an almost unerring delivery. All comedy and humor trade off the inner knowledge we have that any one of us is inevitably returned to the universe of dreams, which mercilessly deconstructs us.

The dreaming experience is rather like being a stupe: the dreamed self is an everyman. No one who enjoys dream life could ever be without a sense of humor.

Humor borrows the naïve fate of the dream subject caught up in a world he should know how to master by now. The Irish or Polish or Norwegian joke—What does it say at the top of a Polish ladder? Stop!—captures the stupidity of the self but at the same time identifies with the thoughtless movement of the world, incorporating the unthinking into the intentional. The dreaming subject is not the director of a dream but is manipulated like any other element in a theatrical production. He seems indeed to be without subjectivity, proximal to the dumb objects of the inanimate world. "A step lower and strangeness creeps in: perceiving that the world is 'dense,' sensing to what degree a stone is foreign and irreducible to us," writes Camus, "with what intensity nature or a landscape can negate us" (20). This negation is expressed in jokes about very stupid people. When you tell such a joke, your listener may well comment on how dumb it is, and intriguingly this is the very point: it is not only a joke about being dumb but a joke that takes into itself the dumb elements of life and personifies them. Dreams regularly turn us into dummies, lorded over by intelligence that seemingly excludes the dumb from the inclusive possibilities of thought and yet affiliates us with the meaningless meanderings of circumstance.

Comics live very close to trauma. When a stand-up comic goes onstage, it is not at all certain whether he will be the least bit amusing. The audience may hope for this, but they do not know what his fate will be. If his jokes are not good, if his delivery is poor, he will die onstage and everyone knows it. The audience has no obligation to find him comic, and aficionados can be as ruthless in their rejections of comics as those at La Scala are of singers. So the stand-up comic bears almost all the anxiety of the moment within himself. We often see this in the densely fraught tangle of a comic figure's body—like the hunched-over Harlequin of the Middle Ages, or the fidgety spasmatic plasticism of Steve Martin, or the spooked-out-of-his-body demi-dissociate Richard Pryor. But comics can uncoil and threaten to spring on the audience. Molière brought the stage closer to the front rows. His characters fell about, almost falling into the audience or opening up buttons and threatening to pee. Flying spittle dispersed an essence of body over a cringing swath of the audience. Modern comics occasionally threaten to enter the audience; in fact, move among them. Then one can see an immediate transformation within the group; anxiety increases while the comic selects someone for special victimization and remorseless humiliation. Does the object of such humor find the occasion amusing? No. It is rather awful. But, nonetheless, the person will not only smile but often laugh hilariously, be forced by this comic intrusion into cracking up. We are witness then to enforced laughter, as the person is compelled into a false self response.

Whether we find a comic's act or a person's joke or a wit's irony amusing will depend on timing and spacing—on whether the humor occurred at the right time and in a suitable space. Humor relies, as we will see, upon an unconscious sense of time and space, operating on an intersubjective plane. And the humorous act always risks bad timing and improper placing, in this respect allowing the potential for disaster always to be glimpsed.

When we observe a comic moving from the straight self into the shambolic domain of his art form, we take notice of a very special transformation—from the conventional to the bizarre, from the ordinary to the extraordinary, from the manageable to the chaotic. We could see this any night of the week at a comedy club. Well, almost. We might not quite observe it, because we know in advance that the comic is transformed once he is onstage. We haven't had an opportunity to see his ordinary self, to be unsure of what he might do, to suffer the pains and pleasures of being objects in his transformation (if he so transforms). This is a mixed blessing: if he does nothing and is perfectly straight, we are disappointed; if he goes too far, we are terrified. We are, in a certain sense, in his hands.

Fools of the court had a very special function. They could say what they wished, and if they roused anxiety among the courtiers, so be it; at least the anxiety did not follow them outside, beyond the space where they functioned as fools. The fool was a confined being, and I should like to argue that comedy—in stand-up, revue, film, or theater—also has its generic place of representation. It is too dangerous a commodity to be allowed to move beyond its reservation.

Why is it so dangerous?

Could we not envision a world that operated according to comic principles? What if our most valued discourse was free-associative, with everybody at least by their adolescence gifted in saying whatever crossed their minds? What if the prank or practical joke was fair game? What if any response to any question could be construed as humorous? What sort of world would it be? Would it be fun, amusing, entertaining? Well. We don't know, do we. It might be awful—however artful, however privileged. Humor let free like that, rather than incarcerated in jokes, comic performance, the theater, can be dangerous. People would live in considerable anxiety. No one could be taken seriously. Straight speech would be mercilessly deconstructed by double and triple entendres. Since there would be no end to it—an important feature of all comedy—people might die laughing.

Could anyone endure a force loose with such license?

In part, we observe this danger when a performance artist or an active comedian enters the real world and conscripts a hapless audience member to be part of his act. We identify with the latter, with the feeling of being taken from a safe remove from the humorist's turbulent capacities to sudden helplessness in a fate determined by this quixotic other. And we know this is exactly where we often place ourselves, flirting, as it were, with danger. What are we doing when we do this?

I believe we are entering a primary area and encountering a primordial object.

The clown may be our very first other.

Look for yourself.

Watch the mother engage with the baby. If you look at her face, you will see someone who exaggerates human expression—wide-open eyes, a great big smile, lengthened—and goofy—vocalizations, upper body swaying back and forth, head thrown back at a tilt, song and dance.

The literature on mothers emphasizes her holding and containing functions, which soothe the infant, that is for sure. But mothers also transform themselves into figures with exaggerated human characteristics in order to stimulate their babies into smiling and even laughing. While it is frowned on to tickle a baby with a "gitchy gitchy goo," a mother will still stimulate a baby with incremental increases in hilarity, from the moment the baby wakes—"Ah! Look who is awake now!"—gradually to playful pushings of the baby's feet and "Well! Who does he think he is? Who does he think he is? Who does he think he is?"—bringing gurgles, chortles, and laughs.

But whether or not the infant finds Mother amusing will largely depend on her timing and spacing. If the timing is poor and if she comes too close to or too far from the infant, she will not develop his sense of humor. Next time you see a stand-up crisscrossing the stage, watch how he plays with the space, rushing to the edge of the stage as if he were going to propel himself into the front row, retreating back toward the curtain, receding from his manic creations, which seem to hover in mid-stage between himself and his audience. Like the mother timing and spacing her approach to her infant, a comic will uncannily portray one feature of his art more visibly than others, which are incorporated more in the poetics of delivery.

Does a comic approach come too close for comfort? Does it compel laughter, driving a false self into a predetermined response? Or is it just about right, allowing us to identify with it, eliciting our true self's spontaneity? Does the individual ego inherit the mother's sense of timing and spacing? Does any person's construction of a dream partly evolve from an earlier state of being within the other's theater, within the mother's world and then within one's own dream world? Is it a transfer from the unconscious aesthetic of the intersubjective to the poetics of intrapsychic existence?

Anyone doubting the amusement that mother and infant take in each other need only book a place in one of the many psychoanalytic cinemas in town. There you can see films by the Truffauts and Godards of psychoanalysis, feature films by the likes of Stern and Trevarthen and Murray, with mothers and infants by now as famous as Greta and Harpo. Certainly, Charcot's theater at the Salpetrière, closed now for quite some time, has been superseded by the 2001 space lab of an Arthur Clarke world featuring the great baby on the big screen. Some of them are so wired up in their little chairs, hooked into spanking-clean computers registering every one of their gestures, that they resemble the wise founding god that Keir Dullea portrayed, though in contrast to the hysteric's almost sickeningly melodramatic gestures—after a while it must have been just too Hollywood—the baby is a minimalist genius. You have to be on the edge of your seat to grasp his gestural scriptures, the ever so subtle signs of a divinity expressed before the dreary deformations of development close the show.

There is a quiet life-and-death struggle going on: no laughing matter. These psychoanalytic filmmakers are now certain, after making countless features, that all infants suffer from "basic misery" (Bradley, 117). Babies spend on average up to 180 minutes a day crying or fussing during their first three months—almost half the time they are awake! Well might we ask why the baby smiles in the first place—at around two weeks of age—but we can rest assured that it seems to have nothing to do with pleasure and usually occurs first while dreaming. Whether they make it or not out of this misery depends, we gather, on just how hard Mom works to entertain them. Baby presumably finds this amazing entertainer funny. And although he is gassed up, crapped out, wet with his own urine, and immobilized, at least he has something really to laugh about—other than those dream images that cross his mind when he is fortunately taken out of the world into intrapsychic darkness.

However clever infant researchers are in finding an infant's skills, the euphoria surrounding this research is reminiscent of the dolphin mania of the 1960s. An entire generation thought that it was merely a matter of a decade at most before dolphins would speak, write autobiographies about life at sea, move from Sea World to Parliament. Baby worshipping—a kind of mangerophilia—would have us believe that infants are on the verge of a similar breakthrough, but in fact baby *is* rather stupid. He smiles because he does not *know* what a miserable situation he is in. And the Great Clown in the sky knows this; when she puts on "showtime," she is luring him away from his true predicament into the world of make-believe. She believes she's with a sucker who will laugh because he doesn't know better. He is the first true ingenue: too ignorant to know that he is being taken in. Stan Laurel brought such a baby into the adult world and linked him unforgettably to one kind of comic figure: the half-wit who needs a goofy adult (Oliver Hardy) to see him through reality.

Melanie Klein believes that babies don't know at the beginning that the mother who is full of good milk and humor is the same mother who has no more milk and seems wicked. This may be just as well. For the position these two are in is at the very heart of what is humorous, a heart as ancient as farce itself. Clowns, who usually act together, have at the center of their repertoire one figure who is constantly hungry and miserable and another who is bursting with goodies to eat and fulsomely content. "Clowns, like minstrels and 'comics,' always deal with the same problem," writes Dario Fo, "be it hunger for food, for sex, or even for dignity, for identity, for power. The problem they invariably pose is—who's in command, who's the boss?" (172). Thus, in the beginning, does baby *know* that the great clown in the sky is the one with the booty? A breast just brimming with milk? Will she give it up, or is there going to be a food fight? Clowns love to throw food at each other. In fact, according to Brazelton, food fights are a feature of conflict between mother and baby: their " 'tug of war' type of relationship is common; it appears around issues of feeding, toilet training, and discipline. The basic issue is: 'Who is going to dominate whom?' " (152).

Cracking up baby, then, is a useful way to neutralize a power conflict, but mothers break up baby during tranquil times as well.

The mother-infant relation, then, is something of a farce: one person—much the superior in power, treating the other as an equal, though, in fact, the superior one takes pleasure in the inferior one's frailties, which then become endearing. Theatrical comic scenes usually play off just such a difference between any two people: one who is smart and sees something, the other who is a dunce and does not see anything; or one with the goodies (breast) and the other without (open mouth). But as the goodenough mother turns inequality into a pleasure for both participants, she also shows how amusement at one's plight can generate a special sense: the sense of humor. Freud thought of humor as deriving from an intrapsychic position: the loving superior superego taking pleasure in the ego's meanderings. We might add that this intrapsychic inequality owes its structure to the early imbalance of power between infant and adult, between the stupe and the know-it-all. In its origins a sense of humor takes pleasure in inadequacy. A mother who is amused by baby and who can get baby to laugh at himself before he consciously knows what the joke is all about helps to develop a sense of amusement in the human predicament well before the self comprehends his condition. The sense of humor precedes the sense of self.

What other functions does this humoring serve?

If the great clown simply talked to her baby like an adult, what would be lost?

Psychoanalytic literature is full of references to the first other as a mirror. This idea figures prominently in Lacan's, Winnicott's, and Kohut's theories of the origin of the self. For Winnicott and Kohut, the good mother must mirror the infant, giving him back an image of himself that accurately derives from his inner experience: if he is distressed, she soothes him, and in doing so provides him through a changed inner experience with a self that matches her own tranquillity. The differences between self and other—which the infant can cognitively discern—are muddled, for the mirroring mother lures the infant into a kind of merging with her own being, creating within the baby a feeling that his resolution of existential difficulties derives from nascent creative abilities of his own. Thus the great mirror helps the infant, who would otherwise feel chaotic and fragmented, feel integrated and self-assured.

For Lacan, the other-as-mirror gives the infant a false image of himself that creates an illusion of unity; the infant is really in bits and pieces but sees a whole self in the glass and says, "That's me." The mirror, then, is the basis of a split in self-identity which lasts a lifetime.

But what if Lacan's mirror were a funny mirror? One which gave back fragmented images? Cubist images? Distorted images? And what about the mother who mirrors as a clown, who forces the infant out of tranquillity into jocularity, who breaks up baby? What sort of mirroring is this?

We may be able to make sense of this if we keep in mind that the mother metamorphoses from her ordinary facial self into a clown; she breaks herself up in order to break up baby. They crack up together. Has she an uncanny sense, then, not only of mirroring alternate states of quiescence and disturbance but of transforming this potential for psychic disaster into pleasure? Does she take into herself, right before the baby's eyes, that internal madness which shakes up baby—as it were, absorbing and transforming the element of shock and disturbance? Does she do what comics and humorists have been doing all these centuries, taking up into their bodies and souls these disturbing aspects of life?

If so, then the provocative and disturbing mother who cracks up baby is a vivid and moving expression of the marriage of unconscious and circumstantial material. Her surprising, unpredictable attacks of jocularity seem accidental; but if her timing and spacing are good enough, she senses when the clowning is all right for baby, joining subject and existence in an exciting way. Some mothers apparently cannot do this, or the infant lacks humor and cannot sense the spirit of the event, does not catch the clues.

By finding pleasure in the infant's frailty—this is expressed in countless lullabies, like "Rock-a-bye, baby, on the tree top, when the wind blows, the cradle will rock, when the bough breaks, the cradle will fall, and down will come baby, cradle and all"—and by provoking baby to do the same, the mother both relieves herself of ordinary hate and transforms violent feelings into mutual aggression: baby spits up food, urinates, shits, and laughs back; Mommy sings songs of murder and talks of loving the little bundle so much she could gobble it all up. It verges on a Punch and Judy show. Strings attached.

Mom the clown regularly deflates the baby's grandiosity by taking the piss out of him, and baby's laughter disarms the frustrated mom. In all this, the mother is building into the infant's psychic structure that pleasure which is intrinsic to the self's follies, that relief we all need from the tedious demands of a grandiose frame of mind. She transforms potential trauma—reality's rude impingement upon one's imagined life—by turning it into pleasure, and deconstructs the violences of the real into the aggressions of the intersubjective.

In thus developing hers and her infant's sense of humor, a mother brings under temporary human control something that is in fact beyond human influence. Beyond the infant-mother couple, outside the comedy club, is a world of the real that is deeply thoughtless. By clowning, the mother re-presents this world and allows vestiges of trauma to show in the human face, turning plight into pleasure.

Perhaps a sense of humor is essential to human survival.

Amusement in the self and in the other may be a vital constituent part of a comprehensive perspective on life. The mother who develops her baby's sense of humor is assisting him to detach from dire mere existence, from simply being in the rather shitty world of infancy, for example. Such a child can, as an adult, ultimately find humor in the most awful circumstances, benefiting from the origins of the comic sense.

Of course, sadly, this is not always the case. Puppet and clown are not always a transitional Punch and Judy show leading to sensuality, aggression, and the symbolic: they may never be more than two disengaged stiffs.

————

Charlie Chaplin constantly hinted, in his art, at puppetry, using a tradition in which the comic borrows the schizoid postures of the wooden soul. "It has been pointed out that much of the mime and many of the gestures of the Commedia [dell Arte] characters are closely related to the distinctive movement of puppets," writes Dario Fo. "I have been aware of it myself when executing one specific style of walk with swift about-turns where the sudden twist of the leg in the opposite direction is a classical imitation of the puppet twirl. The same could be said for the attempt to give an almost wooden quality to certain gestures, like falling and rising while maintaining a jerky movement of the head and shoulders" (24).

A sense of humor—which takes pleasure in the contradictory movements of two objects (two people, or a person and the environment, or a word and its other meanings) —incorporates the plastic and the wooden, the fluid and the fixed. It captures a strange balance we may have in ourselves between the languid pleasures of being and the stiffening frights of life, between the mother as succulent sensualizing other and the mother as mind-blowing fury, between the father as World Cup coach and the father as Cronus the castrator. A comic position is built into the very structure of our soul, occupying as we do a transitional and a transfixing state, energized as we are by desire and jerked about by fright, both plastic and wooden.

This radical contradiction in our being could become a fateful collision—as with Oedipus, whose spontaneous intuitions were pitted against his appalling stupidity—or the occasion for self-amusement. We may choose, then, between our comic and our tragic potential.

It is interesting that many of the great comic figures of this century—Chaplin, Keaton, Laurel and Hardy, Tati, Allen, Cleese—create characters who are accident-prone, who don't have a clue: that is, people for whom the unconscious is married to circumstances in disastrous ways. They are out of touch with their surroundings, however determined they may be to master their fate. They mirror an initial experience with the great clown in the sky that went wrong, one that married their generative unconscious abilities not with the object world but with wrongmindedness. They are amusing to us because we can't imagine forever getting into such difficulties ourselves, however often we slip up. We all have friends or colleagues who seem to live precariously close to this kind of existence, who seem woefully canny in matching their unconscious destructiveness or anxieties with their circumstances in such a way as to court disaster. Down the road a piece— farther toward Thebes—stands the tragic figure who is so blind that his connection with the real is murderous and will end his life, the ultimately clueless man.

"Mirrors should reflect a little before throwing back images," wrote Cocteau. But often we do not have time for reflection, things are happening too fast, and what we show in response to the other—"Hey, why are you looking at me like that?"—is taken as bad mirroring. Poor black Americans, who may live with the possibility of violent encounter every day of their lives, have cannily evolved a system of remirroring that displaces the bad moment onto others and, at the same time, expresses many of the presumed insults that evoked conflict in the first place. This art form is called "snap." Typically, two combatants spar with one another, but not surprisingly, the mother is the ultimate object of this warfare. "Your mother is so fat, when I got on top of her my ears popped." "Your mother's so fat she has to use a satellite dish as a diaphragm." "Your mother is so fat, after making love to her I roll over twice and I'm still on her." "Your mother is so fat she stepped on the scale and it read, 'Fuck it . . . They don't pay me enough for this.' " Snaps also aim missiles at other members of the family and at the image of the body—"You were so ugly at birth your parents named you Shit Happens"; at unwanted children—"You're so ugly, every time your mother looks at you she says to herself, 'Damn, I should have just given head' "; at poverty—"I went to your house, stepped on a cigarette, and your mother screamed, 'Who turned off the heat?' " If the combatants last it out, one of them invents a snap that breaks it up and the defeated simply walks away in disgust: "Shit, man, you're pathetic." The joke is meant to be so bad that even though it bears an insult it is beneath riposte; conflict thus is averted, for the other is not deemed worthy of losing one's life for or getting into shit for (Percelay et al., passim).

Snapping's versatile ability to voice jocular exchange in the midst of extreme danger is intriguing. Has the mother, in the subtle art of reflecting, been a mirror throwing back images very quickly, stimulating the baby into many dances? Not an individual mother as such, but a mother created by the community, a mother of the mother-fucking world, a mother who, when asked what she's looking at, responds by humorously attacking all the valuables in the other's life. But the other, the attacked family and body, is a community object—a fat mama, a stupid father, a body with a nose too big, a collage of all these that bind the community together. Stand-up comedy here is nose to nose between two adversaries, and in the moment of potentially killing each other they allude to a common family that binds them together.

When one snaps at the other, a boundary is crossed. Conventional discourse is usurped by another language, one that alters those who use it. In a less distinct way, the same occurs when a person tells a joke. He may begin with what appears to be a straightforward account, but at some point the listeners realize that this is now a joke. The joker and the audience enter another place. Even a wry comment slipped in an otherwise serious order will refer to another place that everyone knows about. The ironic comment brushes the shores of another country, a dreamscape where people do not think conventionally and where they live according to different forces.

The comic, the joker, the wit who evoke this force remind their listeners of another world with varying degrees of effectiveness, at different points along a spectrum. The practical joker alters the real world and creates a mad one that traps the unsuspecting soul, a clear victim of this transportation. A wit tampers with the tediums of convention, nudging the others toward quiet rememberings of the other world.

The movement of humor in a comic act disables expectations. This may be intended or unintended. Some people have a natural sense of comic function: they appear to have abandoned any concern with adapting to convention and let themselves loose on the world. People like Ken Kesey, who was always getting himself and others into trouble. Once, for example, he joined a small gathering sponsored by the French Department of Stanford University to celebrate a meeting between Jean Genet and members of the Black Panther Party. Before he arrived, matters were rather tense. The Panthers did not know who Genet was and were also irritated by certain black well-wishers, to the point that one of them—Elmer "Geronimo" Pratt—spit in the face of a man whom he deemed to be an Uncle Tom. Genet's admiring comments—he found the Panthers "authentic"—did not lessen their increasing unease. Kesey arrived like a character from *One Flew Over the Cuckoo's Nest*: a bit smacked on drugs, wearing a silly grin. He shook Genet's hand and flashed a broad grin, revealing a front tooth capped in an enamel American flag. Genet laughed. Kesey then pointed to his socks: "I'm wearing green socks." Genet looked nonplussed. "Green socks. Can you dig it? Green socks. They are heavy, man, very heavy." Genet's translator gave a literal rendering: "Les chaussettes vertes, elles sont très, très lourdes." Genet gathered up some sympathy for Kesey's presumed plight, but then Kesey blurted out, "You know what? I feel like playing basketball. There's nothing better than playing basketball with Negroes. I could go for a little one-on-one with some of these Negroes right now." The Panthers were momentarily struck dumb. One Panther moved toward him threateningly, but their leader, David Hilliard, stopped him: "Stay cool, man. This motherfucker is crazy. This motherfucker is crazy and we're getting the fuck out of here." As they left, Kesey wondered out loud, "Don't they like basketball?" (Collier and Horowitz, p. 13). He quite literally broke up the group.

A satirist may intentionally crack up a group, perhaps none more controversially than Paul Krassner when he was editor of *The Realist*. Several years after the assassination of President Kennedy, Krassner published a savagely satiric account of the ride back from Dallas on Air Force One during which Lyndon Johnson was sworn in. He used as his pretext the recently published book by William Manchester, *Death of a President*, several controversial passages of which, it had been reported, had been deleted. What had they contained? Krassner announced that he was publishing the missing portions in *The Realist* and the following appeared: " 'I'm telling you this for the historical record [says Jackie Kennedy to Manchester] so that people a hundred years from now will know what I had to go through . . . That man was crouching over the corpse . . . breathing hard and moving his body rhythmically. At first I thought he must be performing some mysterious symbolic rite he'd learned from Mexicans or Indians as a boy. And then I realized—there is only one way to say this—he was literally fucking my husband in the throat. In the bullet wound in the front of his throat. He reached a climax and dismounted. I froze. The next thing I remember, he was being sworn in as the new President' " (Krassner, 133).

Publication of this account offended an entire nation. Yet, intriguingly, many people either believed that it was correct—thus bringing into focus their fantasies about Mrs. Kennedy's dislike of Johnson—or could not determine if it was true or not.

Krassner's account was a sick joke, but unlike the traditional sick joke (What did the Angel Gabriel say to Nicole Simpson when she got to heaven? "Your waiter will be right with you"), the *Realist*'s jest failed to warn the audience that a joke was on its way. The humorist tapped the unconscious life of a nation: he was the comic let loose upon the world. Ordinarily, sick jokes, which are quite common following disasters, turn horror into amusement, so that the humor immediately creates a different frame of mind. But to the extent that humor and its agents— comedy, jokes, wit—move us into another universe, they always border on the catastrophic. Any reference to the other side—or the far side—usurps the otherwise privileged place of convention. It takes a certain kind of person engaged in a certain kind of violation to move himself and us across the border to the far side. Comics are in a sense leaders. They lead a group of engagingly unsuspecting souls to another place where the body, life's manners, serious issues, and human characteristics are ruthlessly exposed.

Krassner attacked two Presidents, a former First Lady, and, in effect, the sensibilities of millions of people. The stand-up usually lampoons current public figures or unfortunate souls who are good for a laugh. Billy Connolly, in "Billy Connolly Live 1994," mocked the victims of man-eating viruses, Fred West, the Member of Parliament who accidentally killed himself in intended near-death sex, yoga, men's scrotums, Italian waiters, bomber pilots, smart bombs, Michael Jackson, the Scots, the Swiss, schizoid schoolboys, daytime television, experts of all kinds, restaurants, members of his family.

The "send-up" joke is a kind of gift of the stand-up moment. In the United States, lawyer-bashing jokes are in. "How are a lawyer and semen the same? Both have a chance to become human beings." "Did you know that psychological laboratories are now using lawyers for scientific experimentation, rather than rats? They found that the technicians got less attached to lawyers. And they found there are certain things that rats won't do."

Connolly, Krassner, the send-up comics stage a world mockery, inversions of convention. *Mundus inversus* is an ancient feature of the comic saboteur, practiced since classical times. Donaldson argues that there are three types of comic inversion.

There are, first, those which show strange cosmic upsets: a sun and moon shining together in one sky, fish flying across land, men hunting on horseback across the sea. Then there are those that show reversals in the normal relationships between animals and men: an ox cuts up a butcher who hangs from a hook, fish angle for men, horses groom their masters and ride about on their backs . . . The third category . . . shows reversals in the normal relationships between people: here we see a man holding a baby or a distaff while his wife marches up and down with a stick and gun, a pipe stuck between her teeth; two girls beneath a balcony serenading a bashful man; a wife beating her husband; a daughter breast-feeding her mother; a son teaching his father to read; a client defending his lawyer; a servant putting his master to work. (22–23)

Or a patient charging his psychoanalyst, one might add.

When Eldridge Cleaver ran for President, he called Ronald Reagan "Mickey Mouse." The very sight of a black militant campaigning for this august position and nominating his opponents with Disney names seemed to middle-class Americans as if their world was turning over. Cleaver brilliantly captured the logic of humor: he could not be taken seriously and in this lay his strength. No one quite knew what he was up to, as, indeed, no one quite knows what Ross Perot would turn into—does he know that he is Popeye?—or what world he would create if elected to Pennsylvania Avenue. Oliver North, convicted of perjury, grins his way through an election campaign in Virginia, a twin of another cartoon figure, Alfred E. Neuman of the "What Me Worry?" world of *Mad* magazine. Little wonder that the great American humorists—Twain, Mencken, Will Rogers—found American politics the most sidesplitting show in town. One need only mention Ross or Ollie to feel a joke coming on. Try it. Just say, "Now, about Ross Perot . . ." or, "Want to hear the latest about Ollie North?" and all but the fanatic supporter knows he is inside your humor whether he wishes to be or not. You can feel the anticipation develop.

Laughter often derives from this tension of anticipation, as the listener realizes that the comic is crossing the line, that for a moment he is getting hold of a force from the other side. Stand-up comics actually seem to have gripped the beckoning hilarity. If they manage to hold on to it and speak, then they will deliver *it* in a good way. Or they may be killed by it. Either way, they are interlocutors between a force on the far side and the social milieu. Conductors.

The recipient of a humorous remark has an initial response—"Oh, a joke: ah . . . I know this happening"—but at this point the self unconsciously recognizes someone: "I know this timing and spacing from somewhere . . . I know its effects . . . ah . . . I know you. Clown!"

When two people snap at each other, or when a comic goes onstage before an audience, a question in everyone's mind is whether or not a boundary can be crossed, a force got hold of, its energy used to crack up the other. Energy transferred is always there. Freud gave it the name of instinct, and psychoanalysis for a long time conceptualized it as free-moving energy. So we may say that the force that a humorist grasps when he crosses the boundary is the constant unconscious movement of instinctuality, which is associated with known urges: hunger and the urge to eat or drink, defecation and the urge to eliminate, genital excitement and the urge to fornicate. And so it goes.

These instincts usually determine themselves. They exist whatever the context. But a sense of humor may tap their energy, borrow not only their force but their sources and its aims. The comic moment may be a descent into the underworld, where it dips into the force of instincts and returns with enough energy to split sides.

Is it death-defying? Is this journey to the far side and back a minor triumph of the self, a self that goes to the dark world where humanity is shredded by ruthless humiliations, to the forbidden which gives life but also takes it? Are the court jester's jibe at the king, the stand-up's spitting image of a president, Cleese's mockery of the petty bourgeoisie—are these metonyms of flipping the bird at—we might have to say at God, inasmuch as he fits the image of the one who gives us life and then gives us death.

For a brief moment, then, the funny man defies the forces of life and death. He does deliberately what most of us do by chance. A joke comes to us, or we laugh at something we say, contented recipients of good luck. But the humorist intentionally goes to the world from which humor comes and walks a different path toward the same goal to which the psychoanalyst aspires, toward the world of instinct, into the ribald world of the unconscious, which decimates human intentions, and comes back with something.

They both crack us up.

Lacan clowned it up and embodied in his small theater something true to psychoanalysis—something that seems partly to have come from a powerful otherwhere that disturbs tranquillity. Beadle moves about tricking an unsuspecting population as he deftly manipulates reality to the disadvantage of hapless souls. These actions are rather in the image of our God, aren't they, especially if we see the Bible as a work of comic fiction.

We know, for example, that He was in the beginning a very great gardener. It is not difficult to imagine Him planning and tending Eden, and then inventing man. Nor is it difficult to see how His wonderful place was unfortunately mucked up by human error. We need only imagine a Woody Allen as Adam and a Diane Keaton as Eve—and perhaps Danny DeVito as the Snake—to help us along. We can certainly see the irony of His narcissism as He "created man in the image of himself" only to see what fuck-ups men were.

He seems at times rather woefully out of it. "Who told you you were naked?" He asks of Adam, who hides from Him. "Have you been eating of the tree I forbade you to eat?" He seems to be less omnipotent than His otherwise impressive omniscience makes Him out to be.

When He punishes Eve by giving her pain in childbirth, He reminds one of Ubu—in Jarrès's world: "I will multiply your pains in childbearing, you shall give birth to your children in pain." One can almost hear Him say, "So there!" before stomping off to some less troublesome— inhuman—part of His universe.

When he returns, He seems increasingly bizarre in His retaliations. Irked at the sexual habits of mankind, He decides, "I will rid the earth's face of man, my own creation," and so He announces to Noah that "the end has come of all things of flesh" and from that moment all things are effaced from the earth. After wiping out the earth's populations, however, He smells the fragrance of Noah's burnt offering and changes His mind: "Never again will I curse the earth because of man, because his heart contrives evil from his infancy. Never again will I strike down every living thing as I have done." Whew! Well, thank God for that, eh!

But He does seem to relish tricking his poor creations. Irked now that men speak a common language and indeed are dedicated to building a tower to honor their unity, He apparently thinks to himself, Come, let us go down and confuse their language on the spot so they can no longer understand one another. Whereupon He scatters everyone around the earth with different languages so no one can understand one another. Terrific trick. Imagine if Beadle had the power to cast a spell on a family so that they wake one morning to discover to their horror that they no longer speak the same language; indeed, are founders of a new language and had best create a new world lest they suffer the horrid misfortune of a daily reminder of their essential alienation.

It must have been a mixed blessing indeed for His chosen people to follow Him. Think of the brilliant covenant He hatched—certainly the equivalent of breaking up the language: to command each of the men of His chosen people to cut off part of his penis. "You shall circumcise your foreskin," He tells Abraham. I would have thought that Abraham rather felt the demand acutely and surely suppressed a clarification—"Are you sure about this one?" After all, he had asked for clarifications of previous commands.

Well, we all know the rest of the story, how God went on to do other great deeds, smashing up Sodom, acting as marital counselor to Abraham in his distress with Sarah, ordering Abraham to kill his son.

A God who comes from otherwhere, who has harnessed a power that shakes us, who comes too close for comfort, who plays upon our own incapacity, who presents us a face that presumably exaggerates our own, a clown face, seems a jester who not only puts us into existence but puts us on. If this figure is partly based on the function of the mother—a figure who comes from otherwhere, barely visible, yet audible, who provokes us with her clowning around and shakes us into life—then we may see a line running from God the father, who greets mankind; the mother, who is there to meet us on our arrival; our unconscious, mischievous imp of the soul, which guides us through life; and the comic, who carries on in our midst: infantile, omnipotent, vulnerable, enraging, disturbing, consoling, a figure at once godly and ungodly, maternal and infantile, aware and witless.

Thus does a sense of humor trade on our origins. It dips into a prior age. Something from the back of beyond, the above and below, the "far out," it plays with our reality. All along, humor grasps the absurdity born of human life, launched into existence knowing that "in the beginning is our end." That should be no laughing matter, except perhaps for the gods, who see it coming before we do, and except for our comics, who die our deaths for us so that we may live on, a little bit longer, all the merrier for the sacrifice.

References

Al-Khalil, Samir. *Republic of Fear*. London, 1989; Berkeley, Calif., 1991.
Bataille, Georges. *Eroticism*. 1957. London and N.Y., 1987.
Bion, Wilfred. *Transformations*. 1965. Northvale, N.J., 1965; London, 1984.
Blanchot, Maurice. 1969. *The Infinite Conversation*. Minneapolis, Minn., 1993.
———. "Dreaming, Writing," 1971. In *Nights as Day Days as Night*, edited by Michael Leiris, xix–xxviii. N.Y., 1987.
Bollas, Christopher. *The Shadow of the Object*. London and N.Y., 1987.
———. *Being a Character*. London and N.Y., 1992.
———. *Forces of Destiny*. London and N.Y., 1989.
Brazelton, Terry, and Bertrand Cramer. *The Earliest Relationship*. N.Y. and London, 1990.
Cahill, Tim. *Buried Dreams: Inside the Mind of a Serial Killer*. N.Y., 1986.
Camus, Albert. *The Myth of Sisyphus*. 1942. N.Y. and London, 1975.
Cleese, John, and Connie Booth. "The Psychiatrist." In *Fawlty Towers: The Psychiatrist*. Video. BBC.
Collier, Peter, and David Horowitz. *Destructive Generation*. N.Y., 1989.
Crews, Frederick, ed. *Psychoanalysis and the Literary Process*. Cambridge, Mass., 1970.
Davis, Don. *The Milwaukee Murders*. N.Y., 1991; London, 1992.
Donaldson, Ian. *The World Turned Upside-Down*. N.Y. and London, 1970.
Eliot, T. S. "East Coker." 1944. In *Collected Poems 1909–62*. London and N.Y., 1971.
Federn, Paul. *Ego Psychology and the Psychoses*. 1953. London 1977; N.Y., 1980.
Ferenczi, Sandor. "Psychogenic Anomalies of Voice Production." 1915. In *Further Contributions to the Theory and Technique of Psychoanalysis*. London, 1980.
Fletcher, Angus. *Allegory: The Theory of a Symbolic Mode*. Ithaca, N.Y., 1982.
Fo, Dario. *The Tricks of the Trade*. 1987. N.Y., 1991.

Freud, Sigmund. "Recommendations to Physicians Practising Psychoanalysis." 1912. Standard Edition 12, 111–20; "The Uncanny." 1919. Standard Edition 17, 219–56; "The Unconscious." 1915. Standard Edition 17, 159–215.

Hampshire, Stuart. *Innocence and Experience.* London, 1987.

Heidegger, Martin. *What Is Called Thinking?* Fred D. Wieck and J. Glenn Gray, trans. N.Y., 1968.

Hoffman, Eric von. *Venom in the Blood.* London, 1992.

Holland, Norman. *Poems in Person: An Introduction to the Psychoanalysis of Literature.* N.Y., 1973.

Humes, Edward. *Buried Secrets: A True Story of Serial Murder.* N.Y., 1991.

Jones, Rodney, Charles Sevilla, and Gerald Velmen. *Disorderly Conduct.* N.Y., 1987.

Keenan, Brian. *An Evil Cradling: The Five Year Ordeal of a Hostage.* London and N.Y., 1992.

Kramer, Heinrich, and James Sprenger. *Malleus Maleficarum.* 1486. London and Magnolia, Mass., 1971.

Krassner, Paul. *Confessions of a Raving Unconfined Nut.* N.Y., 1993.

Leverenz, David. "Moby Dick." In *Psychoanalysis and the Literary Process,* Frederick Crews, ed., 66–117. Cambridge, Mass., 1970.

Masters, Brian. *Killing for Company: The Case of Dennis Nilson.* London, 1985; N.Y., 1986.

———. *The Shrine of Jeffrey Dahmer.* London and N.Y., 1993.

Melville, Herman. *Moby-Dick.* 1851. N.Y., 1967.

Milton, John. "Paradise Lost." 1674. *Complete and Major Prose.* London and N.Y., 1957.

Nietzsche, Friedrich. "On the Uses and Disadvantages of History for Life." In *Untimely Meditations,* R. J. Hollingdale, trans., 57–123. Cambridge, Mass., 1983; Cambridge, England, 1984.

Norris, Joel. *Serial Killers: The Growing Menace.* N.Y., 1989; London, 1990.

Nozick, Robert. *Philosophical Explanations.* Cambridge, Mass., 1981; Oxford, 1990.

Percelay, James, Ivey Monteria, and Stephan Dweck. *Snaps.* N.Y., 1994.

Petras, Ross and Kathryn. *The 776 Stupidest Things Ever Said.* N.Y., 1993.

Schiller, Friedrich von. *On the Aesthetic Education of Man.* 1793. N.Y. and Oxford, 1967.

Smirnoff, Victor. "The Masochistic Contract." *International Journal of Psychoanalysis.* Vol 50.

Stern, Daniel. *The Interpersonal World of the Infant.* N.Y., 1985.

Stevens, Wallace. "A Primitive Like an Orb," "The Snow Man," in *Collected Poems.* N.Y., 1954; London, 1995.

Stoker, Bram. *Dracula.* 1897. London and N.Y., 1979.

Timerman, Jacobo. *Prisoner without a Name, Cell without a Number.* 1980. N.Y., 1981; London, 1993.

Waite, Terry. *Taken on Trust.* London and N.Y., 1993.

Wilson, Colin, and Donald Seaman, *The Encyclopedia of Modern Murders.* London, 1980; Avenel, N.J., 1991.

Winnicott, D. W., *Playing and Reality.* London, 1985; N.Y., 1971.

Index